The MAILBOX®

The Education Center®

Arts and Crafts

Ann

BEST OF The MAILBOX® MAGAZINE

The best arts-and-crafts activities from the 1998–2004 issues of *The Mailbox*® magazine

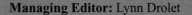

* Easy Art Tips

* Fall Activities

* Winter Activities

* Spring Activities

* Anytime Activities

* Timesaving Index

Managing Editor: Lynn Drolet

Editorial Team: Becky S. Andrews, Kimberley Bruck, Sharon Murphy, Debra Liverman, Diane Badden, Thad H. McLaurin, Karen A. Brudnak, Juli Docimo Blair, Hope Rodgers, Dorothy C. McKinney

Production Team: Lori Z. Henry, Pam Crane, Rebecca Saunders, Chris Curry, Sarah Foreman, Theresa Lewis Goode, Greg D. Rieves, Eliseo De Jesus Santos II, Barry Slate, Donna K. Teal, Zane Williard, Tazmen Carlisle, Kathy Coop, Marsha Heim, Lynette Dickerson, Mark Rainey, Sheila Krill, Laurel Robinson

www.themailbox.com

Manufactured in the United States
10 9 8 7 6 5 4 3 2 1

Table of Contents

Easy Art Tips

Paint Cups

Here's a handy way to recycle those plastic laundry detergent scoops. Use them as paint cups, filling them half full of tempera paint for art projects. Since the scoops have handles, they are easy for little hands to hold and manage. Best of all, they're disposable—no cleanup!

Tiffany Gosseen, Hopkins, MO

Crayon Keeper

No matter how hard you try, it's almost impossible to keep crayon boxes intact for longer than a month or so. The solution? Altoids mint tins. Ask students' families to save these metal boxes for you until you collect a class supply. They're perfect for holding the small pack of eight crayons, and the containers won't tear or get flimsy. What's best, little fingers can better access the crayons than when trying to pull them out of or push them into the original box.

Candace Reid, Greensboro Primary
Greensboro, GA

Cleaning Rubber Stamps

Here's a supersimple way to keep your rubber stamps looking like new! Keep a box of baby wipes handy. After you use a stamp, flip the box open and stamp the top wipe. When the wipe is too dirty to use again (after a few days), just pull out the top wipe and toss it in the trash. Then you're ready to keep cleaning your stamps with the next wipe!

Bonnie Keller, Hazelwood Elementary
Clarksville, TN

Easy Potato Stampers

Making potato stampers is simple with this helpful idea! Cut a large potato in half; then press a metal cookie cutter into the flat side of the potato. Use a sharp knife to cut away about one-half inch of the potato surrounding the cutter. Remove the cookie cutter and you've got a perfect stamper!

Karen Coker
Eastside Elementary
Clinton, SC

Label That Art!

Here's an easy way to label art projects that have hard-to-write-on surfaces. In advance, cut file-folder labels into thirds. Write a different student's name on each section. Then, when a child creates an odd-textured piece of art, simply peel off the appropriate name and stick it to the masterpiece!

Peggy Carr
Lancaster West School
Glasford, IL

Mess Mats

Make art cleanup easy by using these mess mats. Cut a shower curtain into 12" x 24" rectangles. (One shower curtain makes about 15 mats.) Have each youngster place a mess mat underneath his project to catch glue and paint drips. Once the project is finished, simply wipe the mat with a damp sponge.

Kelly Dobias
St. Columba School
Chicago, IL

Spicy Apple Pie

'Tis the season for apples! And you know what that means—freshly baked apple pie! Making these crafty versions of the real thing will fill your classroom with that positively pleasing apple-pie aroma. To make one pie, use a mixture of brown and yellow watercolors to paint the back of a paper plate to resemble the top crust of an apple pie. When the paint is dry, use a marker to draw slits in the center of the pie. If desired, add additional details to the crust. Then squeeze a line of glue along each slit and sprinkle on some apple pie spices, such as cinnamon or nutmeg. When the glue is dry, glue the rim of the crust to the front of another paper plate. Display these tempting works of art on a checkered tablecloth and invite children to use them in their dramatic-play activities. Mmm, can't you almost *taste* it?

Deborah Garmon
Groton, CT

Apple Trees—One Foot Tall

These little apple trees make a big impression on all who see them! In advance, prepare a large container of warm, soapy water for easy cleanup. Have each child cut a treetop from green construction paper and then glue it to the top of a light blue sheet of construction paper as shown. Next, have her step in a shallow pan containing a thin layer of brown paint. To create a tree trunk, help each youngster position her foot on her paper and make a print. Then have her clean her foot with soapy water. Next, have her use a red bingo dauber to print apples on her tree. It's harvesttime!

Diane Bonica
Deer Creek School
Tigard, OR

Johnny Appleseed Hats

Follow up a reading about Johnny Appleseed by making these silvery hats. Provide each youngster with a 7" x 7" piece of tagboard, a 14-inch length of aluminum foil, and a 2½" x 8" piece of black construction paper. Cut a 1½-inch-wide strip of gray construction paper long enough to fit around each child's head and overlap slightly. Then guide each child through the steps below to complete his Johnny Appleseed hat. Hats off to you, Johnny Appleseed!

Directions:

1. Wrap the tagboard square with foil.
2. Cut the black paper into an oval shape to make a handle.
3. Staple the handle to the pot.
4. Staple the headband to the pot.
5. Staple the headband to fit the child's head.

Robin Goddard
Mt. Vernon Elementary
St. Petersburg, FL

Grandparents Day Magnet

This sweet gift will remind grandparents that their grandchildren love them! To prepare, cut a 4" x 6" piece of flesh-toned craft foam in an appropriate color for each child. Cut 1½-inch hearts from red craft foam to make a class supply. Cut magnetic tape into one-inch pieces. Write the provided saying on paper and then photocopy it to make a class set. Have each youngster trace his hand on a piece of craft foam and then cut out the resulting shape. Use a permanent marker to write each child's name on a heart cutout. Instruct the child to attach a piece of magnetic tape to one side of the hand cutout and glue his heart to the center of the other side. If desired, have students make a magnet for each set of grandparents. Have your little ones present the magnets to their grandparents along with the printed notes. Happy Grandparents Day!

adapted from an idea by Susan Page
Thompsontown-Delaware Elementary
Thompsontown, PA

I'm blowing this big kiss your way with a wish for a happy Grandparents Day!

Autumn Leaves

Your youngsters will be delighted to make these dazzling leaf cutouts. In advance, trace and cut out a leaf shape from poster board for each child. Mix equal parts water and vinegar to make about two cups. Cut various colors of tissue paper into one-inch squares. Then have each youngster brush the water and vinegar mixture on the dull side of the leaf to wet the entire shape. Next, have the child place a tissue paper square on the leaf cutout and brush over it with the liquid. Have her continue placing additional tissue paper squares on the wet surface until the leaf shape is entirely covered. Allow the project to dry completely; then brush off the tissue squares. Students will be pleased to see that autumn leaves have arrived!

Debbie Newsome
Dolvin Elementary
Alpharetta, GA

I rake the leaves into a pile,
And then I smile a great big smile!
I jump right in and roll around;
I just love leaves piled on the ground!

In a Pile of Leaves

What's the next best thing to rolling in a pile of real fall leaves? Making a picture of yourself doing just that! To prepare for this project, take your little ones on a nature walk and collect a good supply of small fall leaves. Press the leaves between the pages of a book to flatten them for several days. When the leaves are flat and dry, begin the project by gluing a flesh-toned paper circle to a piece of yellow construction paper for each child. Have each youngster decorate her circle to look like her. Then give her several dry leaves to glue around her face. Add the poem shown to each child's project.

Janette Shoemaker
Prairie View School
Oregon, WI

Fall Hat

You won't "be-leaf" how cute these hats are! To make one, glue two 3" x 12" brown construction paper strips together end to end to make a headband. Label the front center of the headband "Happy Fall!" Next, staple three brown pipe cleaners to the front center of the headband; then add some masking tape over the staples on the back side to avoid scratching. Have each child select three real fall leaves and then tape one to the top of each pipe cleaner. Next, have each child bend the pipe cleaners in various directions to create a pleasing design. Fit each child's headband around his head and staple the ends in place.

Johanna Litts
North Central Elementary
Hermansville, MI

Happy Fall!

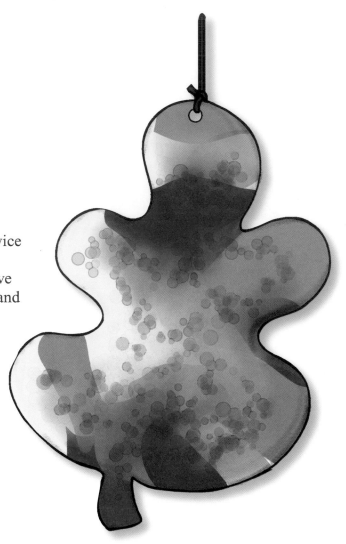

Leaf Suncatcher

Add some whimsy to your windows with this fall project! For each child, lay a piece of clear Con-Tact covering sticky side up on a tabletop. Have each youngster add small pieces of torn tissue paper in fall colors to the covering. Then squirt the paper once or twice with a spray bottle of water to make the tissue colors blend. Once the projects are dry, laminate them and have each child trace a leaf shape onto her laminated paper and cut along the outline. Punch a hole at the top; then use string to hang the suncatcher in a window.

Teresa Harmon
Hillsborough, NC

Jack Frost Magic

This magical art project will turn any frosty frowns upside down! Make the Jack Frost solution by combining one cup of Epsom salt and one cup of water. Bring the mixture to a boil; then let it cool just slightly. Then instruct children to cut out leaves from construction paper. Invite youngsters to paint their leaves with the warm Jack Frost solution, then let the leaves dry overnight. The next day, encourage each child to use other art supplies to create a fall scene on a large sheet of paper. Have him add the finishing touches by gluing on his frosted leaves. Display the finished projects on a board titled "Jack Frost Magic!"

Judy Kelley
Lilja School
Natick, MA

Patch o' Pumpkins

To make a puffy pumpkin, trace and cut out two same-sized pumpkins from sturdy art paper. Sponge-paint one side of one pumpkin with orange paint. (If abilities permit, provide red and yellow paint and have youngsters mix the colors together to create many different shades of orange to use in their work.) Arrange crumpled tissue paper, newspaper, or plastic grocery bags on the unpainted pumpkin. Then position the painted one over the crumpled material and staple or glue the edges together. Next glue on a construction paper stem and a large green pumpkin leaf. Then spiral-cut a green circle to resemble a vine and glue it to the back of the pumpkin. Perch these pretty pumpkins in your classroom patch.

Lori Hamernik
Prairie Farm Elementary
Prairie Farm, WI

Pumpkin Quilt

Ever wonder what to do with all of those leftover pumpkin seeds after a pumpkin exploration? Make this pumpkin pattern quilt! Cut a class supply of pumpkin shapes from orange bulletin board paper. Provide each child with an eight-inch square of tagboard and a handful of dried pumpkin seeds. Have the student arrange the seeds in a pattern on the square and then glue them in place. After the glue has dried, have students alternate gluing the squares and pumpkin cutouts to a length of bulletin board paper as shown. Display the pumpkin quilt and talk about the various patterns. It's quite a quilt!

Jennifer Woods
Alma Primary
Alma, AR

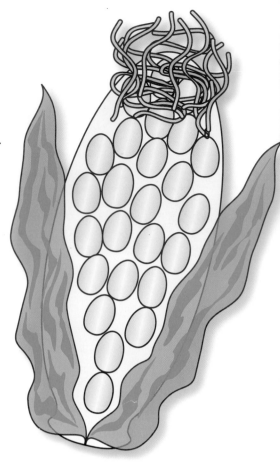

Corn on the Cob

Enjoy eating pistachios? If so, save the shells. They'll come in handy for this fall project. Collect a large supply of pistachio shells. Place the shells in a plastic bag and add a squirt of yellow tempera paint. Seal the bag and then shake it to evenly distribute the paint. Pour the shells onto a tray covered with plastic wrap and allow them to dry. Gather the materials listed below and then help each child follow the directions to complete an ear of corn. It's harvesttime!

Materials for one:
yellow construction paper ear of corn shape
2 pieces of green paper twist (husks)
20–25 yellow pistachio shells (kernels)
dried Spanish moss (corn silk)
glue

Directions:
1. Glue one husk to each side of the ear of corn.
2. Glue kernels to the ear.
3. Glue corn silk to the top of the ear.

Diane Mascola
Noah's Ark Preschool
Hampton, NJ

The Cornfield Crew

Scare up a field of creativity with these cute cornfield characters! In advance, gather a large supply of fabric scraps. Also collect a paper towel tube and a paper lunch bag for each child. To make one scarecrow, stuff the bag with crumpled newspaper; then tie the top closed. Using markers, draw facial features on the bag. Next, cut out scarecrow clothing from the fabric scraps and glue them onto the paper towel tube. (If desired, make simple tracers for children to use to make the scarecrow clothing.) Then use craft glue to attach the bag as shown. Use assorted art supplies—such as large buttons, bandanas, raffia, and construction paper— to add the desired finishing touches. These scarecrow creations look right at home mounted among a field of construction paper cornstalks.

Sheila Crawford
Kids Kampus
Huntington, IN

Discard

Stuff here,
then staple.

Fun Fall Scarecrows

Scare up some fun for fall with these seasonal art projects. Ask each student to bring in a brown paper grocery bag. Cut off the bottom of each bag; then flatten the bag. Fold in the corners; then staple them in place. Have each child gently stuff his scarecrow head with newspaper, then staple the bottom closed and turn the bag over. Invite each child to use art supplies—such as markers, construction paper, raffia, and fabric scraps—to create a scarecrow. Display these finished projects on a bulletin board or around your classroom. They're sure to scare up some classroom fall fun!

Michelle Hall
Biddeford Primary School
Biddeford, ME

Feet and a Treat

Youngsters will step right up to complete this Halloween project! To prepare, print the verse shown onto a sheet of orange construction paper for each child. Paint the bottoms of a child's bare feet with white tempera paint and have him carefully stand on his paper to make prints of his feet. Allow the paint to dry; then have the child use a black marker to add a ghostly face to each footprint. Help him read the verse and ask him to complete the last line by writing or dictating something he'd like to receive when he goes trick-or-treating. Then to complete his paper, have him draw pictures of the treats. "Boo-tiful"!

Kathy Barlow
Southern Elementary
Somerset, KY

Trick or treat!
See my feet!
Here is what I'd like to eat: lollipops

From Plates to Jack-o'-Lanterns

Transform some paper plates and paper into pretty jack-o'-lanterns for Halloween! Gather the materials listed below; then help each child complete the directions to make her jack-o'-lantern.

Materials for one:

two 9" paper plates   black marker
brown construction paper scrap   scissors
green construction paper scrap   glue
yellow and orange crayons

Directions:

1. Color the fronts of the paper plates yellow and the backs orange.
2. On one orange side, draw a jack-o'-lantern face. Cut out the features; then trace around them with a black marker.
3. Cut a stem from brown paper and a leaf from green paper.
4. Glue the edges of the two plates together, orange sides out, with the stem wedged between them at the top.
5. Glue the leaf to the stem.

Jeanine Bulber
St. Mary School
Belleville, IL

Trick-or-Treat Totes

These jack-o'-lanterns show youngsters how to recycle and reuse. Send a note home to parents (and friends and co-workers) asking them to save empty laundry detergent boxes with handles. Collect a box for each child. At one sitting, have each youngster paint her box with glue and cover the glue with torn pieces of orange construction paper. On another day, provide various craft items, such as large wiggle-eye stickers, felt scraps, construction paper, and craft glue. Encourage each child to use the items to create a face on the front of the box. Once the glue is dry, the jack-o'-lantern tote is ready for use.

adapted from an idea by Debbie Scroggins
Francis G. Blair Elementary
East Alton, IL

Halloween Carriers

There's no trick to getting youngsters to make these handy little carriers for classroom work, other papers, and Halloween treats. To make one carrier, paint the bottoms of two paper plates orange. When the paint dries, use black markers or construction paper shapes to add "hall-o-wonderful" faces. Staple the plates together (with the pumpkin faces to the outside), leaving the top half unstapled. Cut a 6" x 2" strip of green construction paper to make a handle. Staple the handle to the inside top of each plate. During October, encourage each child to use her carrier to transport work from school to home. Every once in a while, toss in a few candy treats with children's work, and watch them light up like jack-o'-lanterns.

Nighttime Neighbors

'Tis the season for these nightly neighbors to grace the rafters of your classroom! In advance, photocopy the wing patterns (page 92) onto tagboard; then cut them out to make tracers. To make one bat project, glue two two-inch pom-poms to the center of a nine-inch tagboard moon. Then trace two wing patterns onto construction paper and cut them out. Fold each wing (as shown); then glue just the inside part of each wing next to the body. Add the finishing features by gluing on construction paper ears, two wiggle-eye stickers, and two pipe cleaner legs. Display these beautiful bats high along a classroom wall or hallway.

Sheila Neupauer
Ellwood City Children's Center
Ellwood City, PA

Fold here.

Handy Bat

Put little hands to work creating this adorable bat! In advance, cut a bat body shape for each child from black construction paper. Have each youngster place both hands on a sheet of black construction paper as you trace around them. Cut out the hand shapes; then help the child glue the thumb of each cutout behind the bat body as shown. Next, have him make two white-paint thumbprint eyes and a thumbprint nose on the bat's face. Have him complete his bat by using a white crayon to draw a happy smile!

adapted from an idea by Deb Knott
St. Anne's School
Wabasso, MN

Holiday Magnets

Patterning practice adds the decorative flair to these versatile holiday magnets. To make one, paint one side of a large craft stick. When the paint is dry, create a festive pattern by arranging plastic confetti pieces. Glue each piece of the pattern onto the craft stick. Then attach a length of magnetic tape to the back of the stick. These magnets make great little gifts or seasonal decorations.

Lori Marie Turk
Most Precious Blood School
Walden, NY

A "Can-Do" Turkey

These beautiful birds will make super centerpieces on Thanksgiving tables everywhere! To make one, cover a 14½-ounce can with white construction paper. Next, have a child make a footprint with brown tempera paint on white poster board. When the paint is dry, cut around the outline and glue it to the covered can, toes down, as shown, to represent the turkey's head and neck. Then have the child trace one of his hands three times onto fall colors of construction paper. Have him cut out the hand shapes and glue them to the back of the can to make tail feathers. Finally, have him glue on a yellow construction paper beak, a red paper wattle, and two paper reinforcements for eyes as shown. How gobble, gobble gorgeous!

Kelly Wilkinson
Holy Family School
New Albany, IN

Tabletop Turkey

These colorful turkeys are sure to create a truly festive Thanksgiving table. Gather the materials listed below and then help each child follow the directions to create a tabletop turkey. Gobble, gobble!

Materials for one:

toilet paper tube	red construction
6" paper plate	paper wattle
stapler	paintbrushes
access to brown, red, yellow,	glue
green, and orange paint	black marker
orange construction paper feet	scissors
orange construction paper beak	

Directions:

1. Paint the tube brown and allow it to dry.
2. Paint the plate in four sections, one each of red, yellow, green, and orange. Allow it to dry.
3. Staple the tube to the plate as shown.
4. Glue the feet to the bottom of the tube.
5. Glue the beak and wattle to the front of the tube.
6. Use a marker to add eyes.
7. Cut one-inch slits around the edge of the plate to make feathers.

Susan DeRiso, John W. Horton Elementary, Cranston, RI

A "Spud-tacular" Turkey

Have your little ones waddle on over to the art center to create this printed picture of the big gobbler himself! Cut a potato in half lengthwise and a bell pepper in half crosswise as shown. For the turkey's body, have each child dip the potato into brown paint and make a print in the middle of a large piece of construction paper. Then, for the feathers, have her dip the pepper half into other colors of paint and make prints around the body. When the paint is dry, encourage the child to cut facial features and legs from construction paper and glue them onto her turkey. If desired, laminate the finished prints and use them as placemats.

Kelly Finch
Vaughan Elementary
Powder Springs, GA

An Elegant Table

These pretty place settings serve up big helpings of left and right practice as well as patterning and creativity. In advance, cut a large supply of colorful, one-inch construction paper squares. To make a placemat, glue a pattern of colored squares around the perimeter of a large sheet of construction paper. Next draw or paint your favorite holiday foods on a white paper plate. Glue the plate to the center of the placemat. Fold and staple a napkin on the left side of the plate. Finally, glue a paper or plastic knife and spoon on the right side of the plate, and a fork on the left. Display each child's project on a board titled "A Holiday Table for [number of students in your class]."

Karen Saner
Burns Elementary
Burns, KS

Simple Dream Catchers

Native Americans used them, and with this idea, your little ones can create their own dazzling dream catchers. If desired, share one of the many legends behind the dream catcher before beginning this activity. (Various tales are readily available on the Internet.) Gather colored paper plates (one per child), scissors, a hole puncher, yarn, pony beads, and craft feathers. To prepare, cut the centers out of the plates. Then use the hole puncher to punch holes around the inside of the rims. You'll also need to punch three holes fairly close together on the outside of each rim as shown. Give each child a plate rim and a long piece of yarn.

To make the dream catcher, tie one end of the yarn to one of the holes inside the rim. Then weave the web of the dream catcher by threading the yarn in and out of various holes until all of the holes have been used. If the yarn length gets short, simply tie another yarn piece to it. When the web is complete, knot the yarn through a hole and cut off the excess. Now, tie each of three different lengths of yarn to a separate hole on the outer rim. Thread several pony beads onto each length and then knot the yarn. Finish the dream catcher by inserting the ends of several feathers up into the beads until they are secure. Sweet dreams!

Betty Silkunas, Lower Gwynedd Elementary
North Wales, PA

Native American Patterned Bags

Your youngsters can learn to use patterns as creatively as Native American craftsmen when they make these shoulder bags. Ask parent volunteers to help cut out a class supply of felt shapes using pattern block templates. Give each child two sheets of felt and a two-foot length of cord. Instruct her to glue along three edges of one felt sheet, then press the two felt pieces together. Invite each child to choose felt shapes to form a pattern on her bag. Have her arrange the pattern, check her work, and then glue the shapes in place. After the glue dries, punch a hole in the upper right- and left-hand corners of the cloth. Thread the cord through each hole and tie a knot to secure it in place. Display these bags on a bulletin board during the month of November.

Janet S. Witmer
Harrisburg, PA

Knock, Knock

Who's there? A festive, child-made doorknob hanger that's just right for holiday gift giving.

Materials for one:
one 14" length of wide ribbon
one 14" length of narrow ribbon
dried apple slices
cinnamon sticks
pre-tied red, green, and white bows
scissors
craft glue

To make a doorknob hanger, cut an upside-down V out of one end of the wide ribbon. To make a hanging loop, fold the straight end of that ribbon over the narrow ribbon as shown. Then glue the wide ribbon in place. Next arrange and glue on apple slices, cinnamon sticks, and bows. When the glue is dry, encourage youngsters to choose recipients for their beautiful banners.

Anne M. Cromwell-Gapp
Connecticut Valley Child Care Center
Claremont, NH

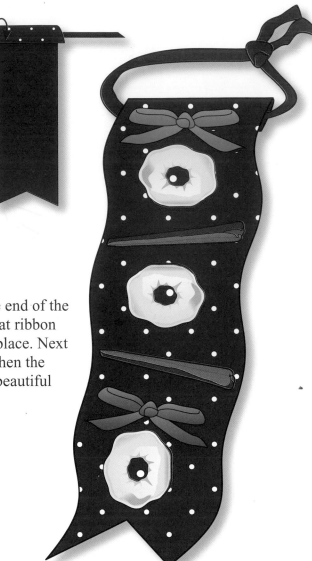

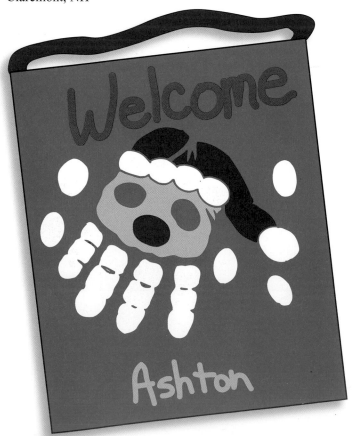

Santa's "Hand-y" Welcome

These festive welcome signs will grace doors for years to come! To make one, use red, peach, and white fabric paint to paint a child's hand as shown. Have the child make a handprint on the center of a dark felt square. Then have him add blue fingerprint eyes and a red fingerprint nose to the Santa's face, as well as dots of white snow around the Santa. Help the child use a fabric-paint squeeze bottle to write "Welcome" above the Santa and his name below. Glue a craft stick along the top edge on the back. Then glue the ends of a length of ribbon to the two top corners for hanging.

Dorothy Lehto
Wise Owl Preschool
Nashua, NH

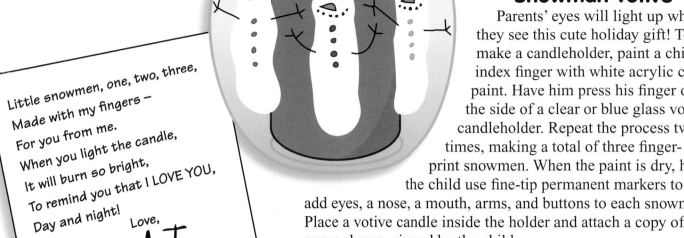

Little snowmen, one, two, three,
Made with my fingers –
For you from me.
When you light the candle,
It will burn so bright,
To remind you that I LOVE YOU,
Day and night!

Love,

A.J.

2007

Snowman Votive

Parents' eyes will light up when they see this cute holiday gift! To make a candleholder, paint a child's index finger with white acrylic craft paint. Have him press his finger onto the side of a clear or blue glass votive candleholder. Repeat the process two times, making a total of three fingerprint snowmen. When the paint is dry, have the child use fine-tip permanent markers to add eyes, a nose, a mouth, arms, and buttons to each snowman. Place a votive candle inside the holder and attach a copy of the poem shown, signed by the child.

Denise Fischer
William Bryant Elementary
Blue Springs, MO

Frosty Frame

Send home a photo in this merry frame! To make one, cut a 4" x 4" square of craft foam. Cut out the center of the square or, if desired, die-cut the center of the square with a holiday design, such as an evergreen tree. To decorate the frame, have a child paint a wooden ice-cream spoon with white tempera paint. Have her use glitter glue to add eyes, a nose, a mouth, and buttons to the spoon snowman. Then have her glue on a top hat cut from craft foam. Use hot glue to attach the finished snowman to one corner of the craft-foam frame. Glue or tape the child's photo to the back of the frame so that it shows through the opening. Then add strips of magnetic tape to the back, or punch a hole in the top and add a loop of ribbon for hanging. Too cute!

adapted from ideas by
Stacey Helders-Peran
Prince of Peace School
Milwaukee, WI

Kris Rangel
St. John's School
Glenwood City, WI

Felicia
2007

Molding to the Music

Engage the whole brain with this process-art activity. Scent a batch of homemade play dough with peppermint oil. Give each child some play dough and turn on some holiday music! While the song is playing, encourage each youngster to use the play dough to form an object or design that expresses how he "sees" the song. When the music stops, give youngsters an opportunity to tell about their works of art. Then start again with a different song.

adapted from an idea by Jennifer Stinnett
Arlington Elementary
Arlington, TN

A Great Plate!

This holiday plate is as much fun to create as it will be to give to a special relative or friend! Each child will need two clear plastic seven-inch party plates. You'll also need to provide access to several different colors of tempera paints that have been mixed with a little glue.

To make the project, drop several blobs of paint onto one of the plates, not too close to the edge. Then place the other plate on top of the plate with paints and squeeze them together. If desired, twist the top plate slightly as you squeeze. Wipe up any paint that extrudes from the edges. Then allow the paint-glue mixture to dry overnight. Place several holiday cookies on the plate and wrap it all in plastic wrap. Finally, attach a card signed by the plate maker. What a sweet gift!

adapted from an idea by Bonnie Elizabeth Vontz
Cheshire Country Day School
Milldale, CT

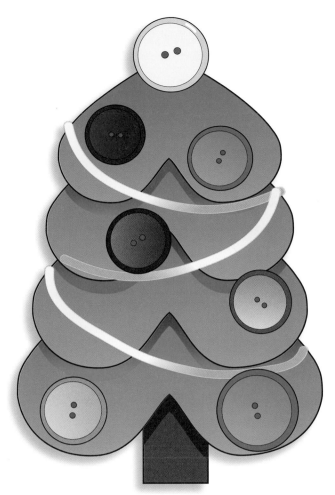

Oh, Christmas Tree!

Warm lots of hearts with this shapely tree. In advance, cut out a class supply each of four different-sized hearts from green construction paper and a class supply of brown construction paper rectangles. Distribute a rectangle and one heart of each size to each child. Instruct the child to find the largest heart, turn it upside down, and glue it to one end of the rectangle. Then direct her to find the next largest heart, turn it upside down, and glue it over the point of the first heart. Have her continue in this manner with the other two hearts. To decorate the tree, invite the child to glue on a variety of craft materials, such as large buttons, foil pieces, ribbons, and tissue paper. Or send the trees home and encourage each family to decorate its tree in a special way. Then have them return the trees for a "tree-rific" display.

Carol Ann Bloom
State College, PA

Light Up the Tree

Christmas trees glow when your little ones make this pretty project! To prepare, cut a symmetrical tree shape from green construction paper for each child. Fold each cutout in half and hole-punch around it. Cut various colors of tissue paper into one-inch squares. Thin a small amount of glue with water for each child. Have each student unfold his tree and brush the glue and water mixture over one side of the cutout. Then have him place tissue paper squares over the holes. After the trees have dried, display them in a window with the tissue paper side against the glass. When the sun shines, these trees will light up your classroom!

Melissa L. Mapes
Little People Land Preschool
St. Petersburg, FL

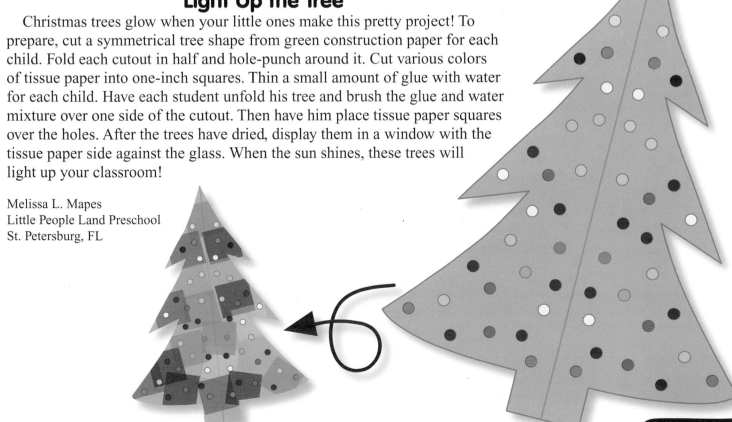

Artichoke Trees

Are you interested in a new tree-printing activity? Try using swirly artichokes! To make one printer, slice off the top of an artichoke, leaving the stem end intact. Place several folded, damp paper towels in a shallow tray and spread green tempera paint on them. Dip the artichoke in the paint. Center the first print near the top of a large sheet of construction paper. Then create a triangle tree shape by making two prints in the second row, three prints in the third row, and so on. Paint or color a brown trunk at the bottom of the tree. When the paint is dry, use art supplies (such as pom-poms, ribbon, and lace) to add festive touches to the tree. Then display a forest of these terrific trees!

Sandie Bolze
Verne W. Critz Primary School
East Patchogue, NY

Colorful Crayon Trees

Crayons on the Christmas tree? Sure! To begin, have each child trace a Christmas tree shape onto the center of a sheet of green construction paper and then cut it out. Have her set the outline aside. Next, instruct each child to use a pencil sharpener to shave old crayons, catching the shavings on a piece of waxed paper laid on the table. When the child is finished, have her fold the waxed paper. Place the waxed paper between layers of brown paper grocery bags on an ironing board. Then use a warm iron to press the paper and melt the crayon shavings for each child. When the paper cools, have the student trim it to fit behind the tree opening on her green paper and then glue it in place. Display the trees on a sunny window to create a festive holiday scene.

Maribeth Foster
Longview, WA

Picturesque Poinsettias

Brighten your classroom and enhance fine-motor skills with these pretty poinsettias. First paint a large sheet of manila paper with red tempera paint. To create bracts (the red petal-like leaves), tear the dried paper into petal shapes. Arrange the bracts on the back of a small paper plate; then glue them in place. Next glue popcorn kernel cutouts in the center. Add torn green construction paper leaves for a finishing touch.

To vary this activity, glue torn red tissue paper pieces onto a white construction paper background; then add green tissue paper leaves. Decorate the center section by squeezing on dabs of neon-yellow-colored glue. Display these holiday beauties in your classroom. It's beginning to look a lot like Christmas!

Julie Robinson
Club Boulevard Humanities Magnet
Durham, NC

Cristie Bagwell
Robert Lee Elementary
Robert Lee, TX

Nifty Nutcracker Hat

Your students will march right over to make this holiday head-band! In advance, cut a class supply of thin white paper plates as shown, keeping the rim pieces. Also, for each child, trim an 8" x 8" square of blue construction paper to resemble the top of a nutcracker's hat as shown. To complete the project, have each child draw a nutcracker face and several curls of hair on the white paper plate. Staple the blue hat piece to the nutcracker's head. Then lay a rim piece across the bottom of the hat and cut the rim to fit. Staple the rim in place and have the child color it red. Instruct him to tape two bright craft feathers to the blue hat piece; then have him add a fancy gold-seal sticker. Attach the nutcracker face to a sentence-strip headband and staple the band to fit the child's head. This nutcracker is ready to wear!

Diane Gilliam
Virginia Beach, VA

Musical Paper Angel

This singing angel is la-la-la-lovely! Gather the materials listed below and then guide each child to follow the directions to complete her angel.

Materials for one:

paper cup

sheet music paper (cut to fit around the cup)

Styrofoam ball

tape

paper doily (cut in half)

pink tissue paper squares

glue

markers

yarn

small bow

Directions:

1. Turn the paper cup upside down. Wrap the music paper around the cup and tape the edges in place.
2. Tape two doily halves to the back of the cup to create wings.
3. Glue the tissue paper squares onto the Styrofoam ball, covering it completely.
4. Use markers to draw eyes and a mouth on the Styrofoam ball.
5. Glue yarn to the ball to resemble the angel's hair.
6. Glue the head to the bottom of the cup.
7. Glue the bow below the head.

Carol Ann Bloom
State College, PA

Lovely Angels

To make an angel, start with one red heart-shaped doily. Make an angel robe by gluing half a coffee filter horizontally across the center of the doily, covering the point of the heart. To make the head, trace a juice-can lid onto any color of skin-toned construction paper; then cut it out. Draw facial features on this cutout; then glue it near the top of the doily so that it slightly overlaps the robe. Hot-glue a garland halo to the very top of the angel's head. Accordion-fold two tagboard arms and glue them to the back of the doily; then wrap them around the front. Then tape a construction paper songbook or a small holiday treat in the angel's hands.

Lori Hamernik
Prairie Farm Elementary
Prairie Farm, WI

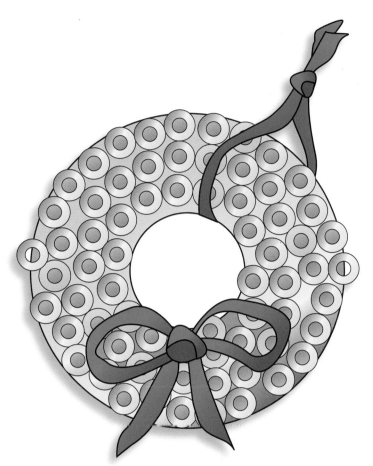

Cheery Cheerios!

Check out these cheerful child-made Cheerios wreaths! Give each child a tagboard wreath cutout. Then have her glue Cheerios to the front and back of her wreath. When the glue is dry, invite each child to paint her wreath to reflect the holiday or occasion she desires. (For example, a child might paint her wreath blue and gold to celebrate Hanukkah, red and green for Christmas, or even your school colors to celebrate school spirit.) When the paint is dry, use craft glue to attach a pre-tied bow. Then tie a length of colorful yarn through the middle hole to make a hanger. Invite your youngsters to use their wreaths to deck the halls and walls of your school.

Lori E. Walter
Roosevelt School
Lodi, NJ

"Hand-some" Santa Hangers

Here's a "hand-some" holiday decoration that little hands will be eager to create. To make one, trace your hand onto white tagboard; then carefully cut it out. Turn the cutout upside down (as shown); then draw a line from the base of the thumb across the palm to distinguish the hat area. Draw a Santa face in the palm area; then color the hat. Next glue one cotton ball to the tip of the hat and a stretched-out cotton ball (or two) across the forehead area. For Santa's beard, glue several stretched-out cotton balls on the fingers. Embellish Santa's hat with glitter or holiday confetti, if desired. When each project is dry, punch a hole at the top and tie on a ribbon hanger. Ho, ho, ho!

Kelly Dobias
St. Columba School
Chicago, IL

Heart in Hand

This lovely holiday ornament is a lasting keepsake. To make one ornament, cut two identical mitten shapes from white felt. (Be sure the cutouts are large enough for a child's hand to fit inside them.) Next help a child paint her hand with green paint, then press it onto one mitten. When the handprint is dry, have the child cut out a small, red felt heart. Hot-glue the heart in the center of the handprint; then also glue the edges of the mittens together except the wrists. Have the child use a paint pen to write her name and the year on the back of the mitten. When the paint is dry, punch a small hole in the top and attach a ribbon for hanging. These precious ornaments are perfect for very special holiday gift giving.

Kathy Martin
Nellie Reed Elementary
Vernon, MI

Earth-Friendly Ornament

Make these cute elf ornaments from recycled CDs and plastic newspaper sacks! To make one, fold down the open edge of a newspaper sack two times to make a cuff. Spread white glue on the printed side of a CD; then slip it into the open end of the sack as shown. After the glue dries, tie the other end of the sack with a short length of yarn; then have a child use scissors to fringe-cut the end of the resulting elf's hat. Instruct him to add paper-reinforcement eyes and glue on a pom-pom nose. Then have him draw a smile with a permanent marker. Tie another length of yarn around the yarn on the hat; then tie the loose ends together to make a loop for hanging.

Dianne Young
Seymour Elementary
Ralston, NE

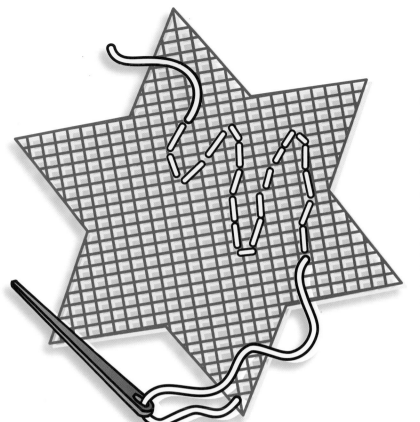

Art "Sew" Easy

Students will stitch these ornaments in a snap! Purchase some large-mesh plastic canvas and several plastic sewing needles with large eyes at your local craft store. Also gather bright or glittery yarns in holiday colors. Cut the plastic canvas into holiday shapes, such as candy canes, stars, snowmen, and trees. Work with a few children at a time, and have each of them choose a shape, as well as some yarn. Help each youngster thread her needle and demonstrate how to begin sewing, weaving the yarn in and out of the holes in the canvas. Then stand back and watch little ones go, go, go as they sew, sew, sew! Add a hook and this ornament's ready for hanging!

Bonnie McKenzie
Cheshire Country Day School
Cheshire, CT

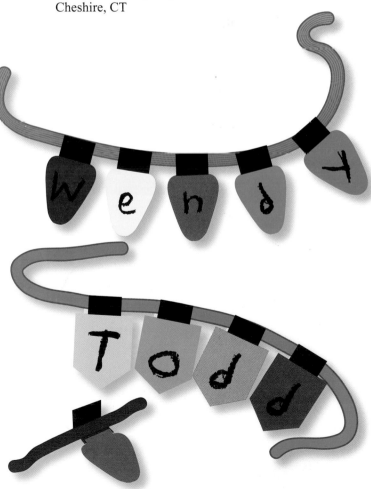

Put Your Name in Lights

Since little ones love seeing their names in print, they'll be thrilled to make—and show off!—this garland. In advance, use the lightbulb patterns (page 93) to make a class supply of tagboard lightbulb tracers. (If desired, dreidel patterns are also provided.) Then cut a 30-inch length of yarn for each student and a large supply of black 1" x 2" construction paper strips. To begin, provide each child with colorful construction paper choices, a lightbulb (and/or dreidel) pattern, and the length of yarn. Instruct each child to trace the pattern one time for each letter in her name, then cut out all the patterns. For each bulb, have each child fold a black paper strip (a socket) over the yarn, insert the bulb, and glue it shut. (Follow the same procedure for the dreidel option using the black paper strip as the dreidel's handle.) Next have each child write one letter of her name (in order) on each light or dreidel. During the holidays, encourage children to display these nifty strands of garland.

Wendy Svenstrup
St. Mary's Preschool
Lafayette, IN

Twinkling Stars

It doesn't have to be nighttime for beautiful stars to appear. Complete this easy craft to add starry sparkle to your classroom decor. To prepare, cut two triangles, equal in size, from poster board for each child. Cut a supply of gold tissue paper into one-inch squares. Then cut a six-inch length of yarn for each child.

Have each youngster glue one triangle on top of the other one as shown. Instruct the child to crumple pieces of tissue paper and then glue them to his star. Invite him to add sparkle accents by squeezing drops of glitter glue on his star. Allow the projects to dry. Hole-punch each star and attach a length of yarn to make a hanger. Twinkle, twinkle!

Deborah Garmon
Groton, CT

Shiny Candle

Light up the holiday season with these shimmering candles! Gather the materials listed below and guide each child through the directions to make a festive candle.

Materials needed for one candle:
toilet paper tube
piece of aluminum foil
3" square of red tissue paper
6" length of Christmas garland
glue

Directions:
1. Wrap foil around the tube and then tuck the excess into each end.
2. Twist the tissue paper into a flame shape and glue it to one end of the tube.
3. Glue a length of garland around the base of the candle.

Anne M. Cromwell-Gapp
Connecticut Valley Child Care Center
Claremont, NH

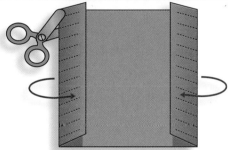

Kwanzaa Mats

If your class is studying Kwanzaa, celebrate these special days by making *mkekas* (traditional woven mats that represent a firm foundation and tradition). In advance, collect one brown grocery bag for every two children. To prepare, cut a supply of colorful, 1" x 18" construction paper strips. Then cut out the large front and back panels of each bag. For each panel, fold in two inches on each short side. Cut the folded sections for weaving (as shown). To begin the activity, give one panel to each child. Instruct her to draw a picture of her firm foundation—her entire family. Then show each child how to weave the paper strips, in and out, on each side of the mat, and then trim and glue the ends of each strip to the mat. Laminate the finished mkekas; then use them as placemats or for other Kwanzaa-related activities. Happy Kwanzaa!

Marvelous Mazao

Habari gani? (What's the news?) *Umoja!* (Unity!) If you're celebrating this first principle of Kwanzaa, try your hands at making a *mazao*—a straw basket of fruit—which is the traditional symbol for this principle. To begin, cut out a basket shape from butcher paper. If desired, use a marker to add details to the basket; then glue it to a construction paper background. Next use a variety of halved and whole fruits and vegetables and colorful paints to make prints on a sheet of art paper. When the paint is dry, cut out each print and glue it "in" the straw basket. Display each child's marvelous mazao during the seven days of Kwanzaa.

adapted from an idea by Carmen Carpenter
Highland Preschool
Raleigh, NC

Winter in a Jar

Little ones will love making their very own snow globes to celebrate the winter season! Collect a clean plastic jar with a lid for every child. To make a snow globe, squeeze waterproof glue into each jar lid. Have each child attach small trees, snowmen, or other appropriate figures found at your craft store to the inside of a jar lid. Then allow the glue to dry. Next, have him fill his jar nearly full with water and add a bit of confetti or glitter. Then use more waterproof glue to coat the inside rim of the lid before screwing it in place. When the glue is dry, invite each child to shake his jar and watch the beautiful scene inside!

Darla Cricchio
Sims Elementary
Bridge City, TX

Shimmering Snowflake

A stencil makes this snowflake a cinch! To prepare, duplicate the snowflake stencil pattern on page 94 on tagboard. Cut out the outer circle; then laminate the stencil. Use an X-acto knife to carefully cut out the snowflake pattern in the center of the stencil.

Place the stencil in the center of an uncoated nine-inch paper plate. To ensure the stencil stays in place during use, use pushpins to attach the plate and stencil to a bulletin board within students' reach. Have each child select a bingo dauber and use it to dab color on the stencil to make a snowflake on her plate. Next, remove the plate and stencil from the wall. Invite the child to use glitter glue to add sparkly accents to her snowflake. Finally, punch a hole near the edge of the plate and add a loop of ribbon for hanging. Look, a beautiful blizzard has just blown into your classroom!

adapted from an idea by Kari Zimmerman
Juda School
Juda, WI

Salty Winter Art

Beautiful snow scenes are in your classroom forecast! Provide each student with a 12" x 18" sheet of dark blue construction paper and three to four tree cutouts cut from green construction paper. Have the child use chalk to draw and color a snowdrift along the bottom of the paper. Then instruct her to glue the trees to her scene. Have her apply glue with her finger to the snowdrift, the ends of the tree branches, and in various spots in the sky. Next, invite her to sprinkle salt over the glue; then help her shake off the excess. Allow the projects to dry. Display the sparkly scenes on a bulletin board titled "Winter Wonderland!"

adapted from ideas by
Dianne Neumann   Ann N. Seal
F. C. Whiteley School   Verona Jr. High School
Hoffman Estates, IL   Tupelo, MI

Sweet Snowmen

It's fun to make these sweet, little snow creations—and they won't melt in your classroom! Begin with a blue construction paper background. Use dabs of white glue and large marshmallows to build a snowman on the paper. Then poke in toothpicks to resemble arms. Add details with fine-tipped permanent markers and construction paper scraps. Then complete the scene by gluing small marshmallows in the sky and on the ground. (Remember to have extra marshmallows on hand for snacking!) When the glue is dry, display the finished projects with a banner that reads "We're 'SNOW' Glad to Be Here!"

Martha Ann Davis
Springfield Elementary
Greenwood, SC

Scissors to Snowman

Snip your way to this snazzy snowman—he's easy to make! Fold up one long edge of a sheet of 9" x 12" white construction paper about 3½ inches. Use scissors to cut slits about an inch apart along the fold, being careful not to cut all the way to the edge of the paper. Unfold the paper; then roll it from one short end to the other to create a tube. Glue the paper in place. Have each child use a black marker to add eyes and a mouth. Instruct him to glue on a nose cut from orange construction paper. Then have him cut a long strip of construction paper in any color and glue it around the neck of his snowman to form a scarf, allowing the ends to stick out. Finally, help each child thread a length of yarn through two holes punched in the top of the snowman. Tie the yarn into a loop, and hang the snowman to display.

Johanna Litts
North Central Elementary
Hermansville, MI

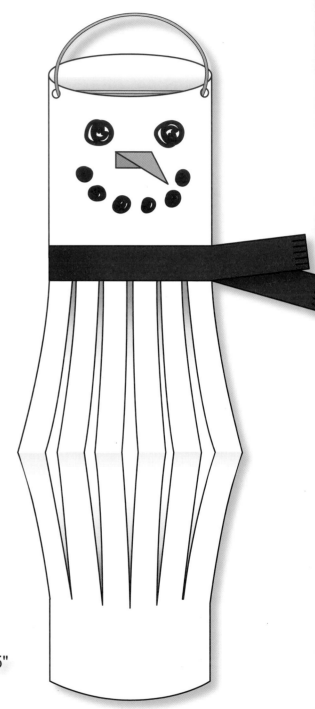

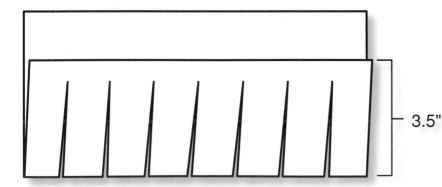

3.5"

Blowing in the Wind

Perk up those wintry windy days with these snowman windsocks. For each child, duplicate page 95 on white construction paper. Provide craft glue and a variety of craft supplies, such as fabric scraps, large buttons, pipe cleaners, and crayons. To make a snowman windsock, cut out the pattern. Use the craft supplies to decorate the middle of the white portion to resemble a snowman. After the glue dries, cut along the white dotted lines on the pattern. (Do not cut past the dotted lines!) Then form the snowman's hat and body into a cylinder and staple it closed. Gently pull out the cut sections to resemble the brim of the snowman's hat. Add desired details such as a fabric scarf and pipe cleaner arms (poked in). Glue crepe paper streamers to the bottom of the snowman. Finally, make a hanger by punching a hole in each side of the hat and attaching a length of yarn. Display these wintry little fellows where they might catch a current of air every now and then.

Sharon Johnson
Guardino Elementary
Clayton, NY

Milk Bottle Snowman

Enlist the help of parents in collecting a class supply of clean, small milk bottles (about 4½ inches tall), similar to the one shown. Also ask for donations of old, colorful socks. To prepare, remove the lid and label from each bottle. Help each child squeeze craft glue around the mouth of the bottle and then place a two-inch Styrofoam ball over the opening. Allow the glue to dry overnight. To make hats, cut each sock two inches from the toe end. To make scarves, cut the sock into strips. Have each student wrap a brown pipe cleaner around the neck of his bottle to make arms. Provide each child with two two-inch pipe cleaner pieces to wrap around each arm to make hands. Have each child use permanent markers to add a face to his snowman. Allow each child to select a hat and scarf. Help him place the hat on his snowman's head and tie the scarf around his neck. Cute frosty friends!

Brenda Lewis Saunders
Beale Elementary
Gallipolis Ferry, WV

Chocolate MILK

It's a Whiteout!

Your children will have creative fun designing their own versions of this project! In advance, photocopy the bear patterns on page 96. Then use those patterns to make stencils, tracers, and sponge cutouts. (If available, you could also use bear-shaped cookie cutters.) Provide wiggle-eye stickers, black markers, and a supply of white craft items, such as paint, doily scraps, large buttons, and packing pieces. Give each child a sheet of blue construction paper. Then invite her to use the supplies to create an all-white blizzard scene. (Instruct her to leave a little space on the bottom of her paper.) Then, when the scene is dry, have each child write about her scene on the bottom of the page. Why, couldn't you tell? It's a skating polar bear eating popcorn in a snowstorm!

adapted from an idea by Rita Beiswenger
Crescent Avenue Weekday School
Fort Wayne, IN

Ice Is Nice…

…for penguins! This project uses several art techniques to create an environment straight from the Antarctic. In advance, prepare a mixture of two parts nonmenthol shaving cream and one part white glue. To begin, have each child use various items (see list for suggestions) and white tempera paint to print a snowy blizzard on a 12" x 18" sheet of dark-colored construction paper. Then give each child a spoonful of the shaving cream–glue mixture and have him fingerpaint along the bottom of his paper to create mounds of ice. Finally, provide black, white, and orange construction paper (and small wiggle eyes, if desired) for each child to use in creating torn-paper penguins. Display these icy scenes on a bulletin board or use them as covers for individual books during a study of penguins, the Antarctic, or winter. BRRRRRR!

Items for printing:

thread spools	large buttons
pasta wheels	marker caps
small porcupine balls	cotton swabs
bubble wrap	pom-poms

Lin Attaya
Hodge Elementary
Denton, TX

Penguin Puppets

These petite penguin pals are a perfect winter art project! Collect a class supply of black film canisters. For each penguin, cut two oval wings from black craft foam, an oval tummy from white craft foam, a tiny triangle beak from orange craft foam, and two eyes hole-punched from white craft foam. Have a child use tacky craft glue to attach the foam pieces as shown. Then have her use a marker to add a dot to each eye. Let the glue dry thoroughly; then invite each youngster to slip her penguin over her fingers and take him for a waddle!

Trish Draper
Millarville Community School
Millarville, Alberta, Canada

Special You, Special Me

Martin Luther King Jr. had the dream that all people would be accepted just as they are. How boring our world would be if everyone were the same! Give each child a square piece of paper. Have him illustrate something that makes him special or unique, such as a physical feature, a special ability, or a unique hobby. Mount each picture on a square sheet of colored construction paper that is slightly larger than the drawing. Then arrange the squares on a wall to resemble a quilt. Title the display "Uncovering Diversity!"

Serve Up Some Hearts

Little ones will enjoy making these pretty placemats for your valentine party! To make a placemat, use crayons to draw and heavily color a variety of hearts on a 10" x 16" sheet of white construction paper. (Make sure each heart is covered with a thick coat of crayon wax.) Then paint a thin, red tempera wash over the entire sheet. The crayon wax will resist the paint, leaving delicate hearts on the placemat. When the paint is dry, have each child choose a background color of 12" x 18" construction paper and glue his mat onto it. Laminate the mats for durability if desired. Who's ready to party?

Two Liters of Love!

Two-liter soda bottles make inexpensive and sturdy containers for valentines! To make a valentines holder, cut a clean, empty bottle at the top of the label; then remove the label completely. Hot-glue a wide decorative ribbon over the cut edge of the bottle to protect little fingers. Next, punch two holes on opposite sides of the bottle; then thread a ribbon through the holes and tie a knot at each end to make a handle. Now the bottle is ready for a child to decorate with heart-shaped sponges and tempera paint, paint pens, stickers, and glitter glue. Beautiful!

Kristy Helton
Open Arms Ministry
Vienna, MO

Heart Art

In advance, make a heart frame by cutting out a heart shape from a 9" x 9" construction paper square. Set the frame aside. Next pour a nickel-sized dollop of clear corn syrup near each corner of a 9" x 9" tagboard square. Choose a color or two of food coloring; then add a few drops to the corn syrup. Fingerpaint with the colored corn syrup until the tagboard is covered with a *very thin* layer of syrup. While the syrup is still wet, position the frame on top of it. If desired, sprinkle the wet syrup with glitter or other small craft items. When the syrup is completely dry, display these lovely masterpieces with the title "Art From the Heart."

Tip: Save the heart cutouts (from the frame) to use for other art projects, seasonal manipulatives, or notepaper.

Lola M. Smith
Hilliard, OH

All My Love!

Whether it's for Valentine's Day or just any ol' day, this card gets right down to the heart and toes of the matter! To create one card, fold a large sheet of construction paper in half. Then open the card and make a set of footprints on the right side. While the footprint paint is drying, decorate a doily heart with art supplies, such as glitter, puffy paint, and sequins. Label the heart with the recipient's name; then glue it to the front center of the card. Finish by writing the greeting (as shown) on the card.

Cheri Beckwith
Eagle River, AK

Valentine Collage

These tactile valentines are just right for little hands! In advance, use alcohol mixed with a few drops of food coloring to dye a large quantity of dry pasta shapes (such as rotini, macaroni, and wheel); then spread the pasta on newspaper to dry. To make one collage, spread a thick coat of glue on a small area of a tagboard heart. Arrange dyed pasta and dry white rice on the glue as desired. Continue working until the heart is covered in pleasing designs. When all the heart collages are thoroughly dry, encourage children to give their hearts to sweethearts or other loved ones. What a touching gift!

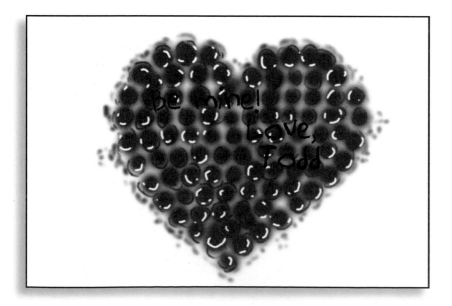

Bubble-Print Hearts

Add a textured twist to making valentines when you use bubble wrap! Tape a piece of bubble wrap to an old cookie sheet. Then have each child paint a heart shape on the wrap. Help him press a sheet of white construction paper onto the wrap to make a print. Then the bubble wrap can be rinsed, dried, and reused by another painter. After each print dries, have the child use a marker to write a special valentine message. When all the bubbly hearts are complete, use them to make a lovely display!

adapted from an idea by Diane Bonica
Deer Creek School
Tigard, OR

Lacy Valentines

Prepare these lacy hearts for your youngsters to embellish in their own special ways.
Ahead of time, laminate a supply of lace.
(Check old fabric-sample books or fabric stores
for discontinued designs.) Use a heart template to
trace hearts onto the lace; then cut them out. Or use
a die-cut machine for quicker cutting. Place the hearts
and a variety of craft materials—such as paint pens,
permanent markers, colored glue, glitter, large buttons,
bows, and pom-poms—in the art center. Invite each youngster to visit the center to create a one-of-a-kind valentine. Use
the valentines for sorting, patterning, or as calendar markers.
Students will be thrilled to use their own creations in learning
important concepts.

adapted from an idea by Brenda S. Beard
Greenbrier Elementary
Greenbrier, TN

A Jar Full of Love

Help your little ones make these fun candy holders to store lots of
hugs and kisses for a special someone. Collect a class supply of small
baby food jars and lids. Then gather the materials listed below. To make a
holder, paint *X*s and *O*s around the jar's sides. While the paint is drying,
place the jar lid in the center of the foil square. Put a few cotton balls
on the lid; then pull the foil's corners up and around the lid. Twist the
foil's edges to create a peak. Poke a hole through the foil on the underside of the lid; then press the foil against the lid's edges. Now fold the
paper strip in half. Print "I Love You!" on half of the strip and then staple
it around the peak as shown. Fill the jar with Hershey's Hugs and Kisses
candies. Then carefully twist on the lid.

Materials needed:
1 small baby food jar and lid (per child)
red paint
1 thin paintbrush
one 7" x 7" square of aluminum foil (per child)
3 cotton balls (per child)
one ½" x 8" strip of white paper (per child)
1 marker
1 handful of Hershey's Hugs and Kisses candies (per child)

Susan DeRiso
John W. Horton School
Cranston, RI

Valentine Keepsake

These valentine keepsakes are sure to make a good impression! Purchase three or four six-inch heart-shaped cake pans and work with three or four children at one time. To make one keepsake, line a cake pan with plastic wrap, working with a large enough piece to leave two inches of wrap hanging over the edges. Mix a batch of plaster of paris according to package directions. Half-fill the pan with the plaster mixture. Before the plaster sets, have each child press her hand into the plaster to make an imprint. Allow the plaster to harden completely; then remove the plaster piece from the pan by pulling up on the plastic wrap. (If necessary, dip the bottom of the pan in hot water.) Have the child paint her heart with red tempera paint, leaving her imprint white. Beautiful!

Beth Wineberger
Southold UFSD
Southold, NY

Hearts and Photos

These seasonal frames are sure to warm parents' hearts! To make one, paint a small wooden frame with pastel tempera paint. Next, use tacky craft glue to attach candy conversation hearts around the frame's opening. When the glue is dry, use school glue to paint over the candy hearts to seal them. When dry, put a picture of the child—sporting a pair of heart-shaped sunglasses—inside the frame!

Lynne Novak
St. Joseph School
Spruce Grove, Alberta, Canada

A Portrait of George

George Washington, that is! Have youngsters make these likenesses of the first president to celebrate Presidents' Day!

Materials for one:
head shape cut from skin-toned construction paper (approximately 6" x 6")
hat shape cut from blue construction paper (6" across the top)
6" strip of yellow construction paper
black and white construction paper scraps
7 cotton balls
red marker
semicircle cut from blue construction paper (7" on the straight side)
half a round 6" paper doily
glue
scissors

Directions:
1. Glue the hat shape onto the top of the head cutout.
2. Glue the yellow strip across the hat as shown; then trim the ends to follow the shape of the hat.
3. Cut two small white circles and two smaller black circles from the construction paper scraps. Glue them together to form two eyes; then glue the eyes to the face.
4. Use the marker to draw a nose and mouth.
5. Glue three cotton balls to each side of the face to make George's wig. Pull one cotton ball into two parts and glue these in place to make eyebrows.
6. Glue the doily atop the blue semicircle; then glue this in place below the chin.

Kathleen Rose
Park Falls Elementary
Park Falls, WI

Log Cabin Creations

Culminate discussions of Abraham Lincoln's birthday and his rustic beginnings with these creative cabins! To prepare, cut a large supply of ½"-wide, brown construction paper strips. To make a log cabin, arrange the strips on a sheet of paper, tearing them as different lengths are needed. Then glue on paper scraps to resemble windows, doors, and other details. To complete the picture, draw in background details with crayons. Abe would be proud of these endearingly rustic cabins!

Susan Logan
Hickory Tree Elementary
St. Cloud, FL

Lincoln's Logs

Encourage your young artists to "build" these cabins in honor of Abraham Lincoln. Have each child glue eight wooden craft sticks to a sheet of white construction paper as shown. Give each child a door precut from brown construction paper, two windows precut from yellow construction paper, and a triangle roof precut from black construction paper. Have each child glue the paper shapes in place, adding details with crayons or markers to the windows, door, and scene as he wishes. Then invite him to finish his project by writing or dictating a sentence about Abe Lincoln at the top of his paper.

Robin Miller
Ganns-Middle Valley School
East Ridge, TN

Lovable Lambs

Youngsters won't mind the March bluster when they have these lovable lambs to remind them that spring is coming! Provide each child with a coffee filter, a large supply of cotton balls, and a sheet of black construction paper. Encourage the child to glue cotton balls onto the inside bottom of the coffee filter. Then have him cut a head, legs, and a tail from the black paper. Have him glue the parts in place, then draw on features with a white crayon. These fuzzy little lambs will help usher in spring weather!

Amy Ross
Community School Age Day Care
Downingtown, PA

Windy Art

As the winds of spring pick up, have your youngsters create these breezy works of art. Provide each child with a sheet of white paper and access to watercolors. Have her paint her entire paper and then allow it to dry. Thin black tempera paint with water. Then give each student a straw. Next, have each child dip one end of her straw in the black paint and let it drip onto her paper. Instruct each child to blow gently through the straw to spread the paint. After the child has completed her painting, have her title it. Display the paintings on a bulletin board titled "Windy Art."

Donna Bishop
Stanley School
Swampscott, MA

Dark Fireworks

Loopy Leprechaun

These charming leprechauns will bring the luck o' the Irish to your classroom! Make several tagboard hat and head tracers similar to the ones shown. Cut twelve 1" x 9" strips from orange construction paper for each child. Provide each youngster with a half sheet of green construction paper (cut lengthwise), a half sheet of flesh-toned construction paper (cut widthwise), a supply of orange strips, glue, scissors, and markers. Help each youngster follow the directions below to complete his leprechaun friend. Then label the leprechaun with the child's name as shown.

To make one:

1. Trace a hat pattern on green construction paper. Cut it out.
2. Trace a head pattern on flesh-toned construction paper. Cut it out.
3. Glue the hat to the straight edge of the head.
4. Draw a face.
5. Glue the strips along the bottom edge of the face.
6. Wrap each strip around a marker to make a curly beard.

Diane Bonica
Deer Creek School
Tigard, OR

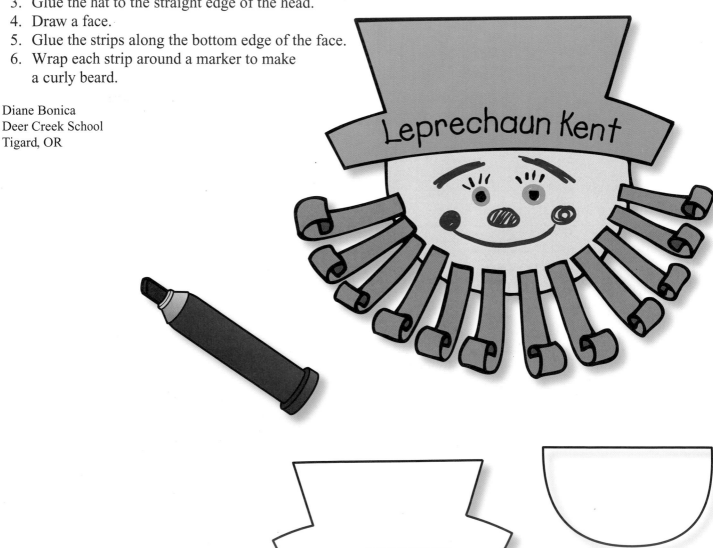

Pouf Painting

Painting gets abstract with this printing procedure! Hot-glue a separate tongue depressor to each of several bath poufs. Pour a different color of paint into separate pie tins; put a pouf in each tin. Give each youngster a large sheet of white construction paper. Encourage him to use the poufs for painting and printing. Once the paint dries, have the youngster trace a seasonal shape onto his paper and then cut it out. Or mount the painting on a larger piece of colored paper and enjoy the abstract masterpiece as is.

Anna Majorie
Allemands Elementary
Des Allemands, LA

Ping-Pong Ball–Painted Shamrocks

Marble painting is always fun, but why not try something a bit different? Put a large piece of construction paper in a box with a lid. Use a plastic spoon to drizzle different shades of green paint onto the paper. Invite a child to drop a Ping-Pong ball into the box, put on the lid, and give the box a few good shakes to make the ball bounce! After the paint has dried, have each student trace a large shamrock on her paper and then cut it out. Use the shapes to decorate your room for St. Patrick's Day.

Jill Davis
Kendall-Whittier Elementary
Tulsa, OK

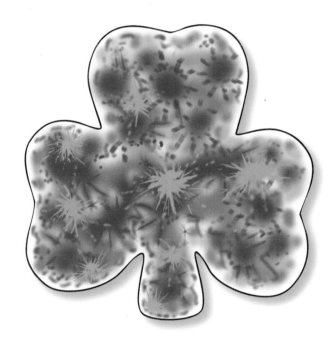

Top o' the Rainbow

To make a windsock, photocopy the hat pattern (page 97) two times onto green construction paper. Cut out the hats and decorate them as desired. Then apply glue just around the side edges of the back of one hat. Press the hats together, leaving the top and bottom edges unglued. When the glue is dry, bend a 3" x 10" strip of tagboard to form a cylinder and then staple it together. Gently slide the cylinder into the hat, creating a rounded, 3-D look. Next glue each of six colorful streamers to the inside bottom of the hat. Attach a shamrock cutout to the bottom of each streamer. Punch a hole in each side of the top of the hat; then tie a length of yarn to the holes. Suspend these windy wonders in an area of your classroom that is likely to receive a gentle breeze every now and then.

D. Hautala
Washington Elementary
Ely, MN

glue

Rainbow Spirals

Celebrate the coming of spring with these spirals! To make one, have a child paint both sides of a thin white paper plate with many different colors of watercolor paint. Encourage her to completely cover one side with colorful designs, allow it to dry, and then completely cover the other side. To make the spiral, begin cutting at the outer edge of the plate, and cut a continuous strip (about an inch wide) until you reach the center. Punch a hole in the center end of the spiral, and then thread a length of yarn through it. Tie the yarn into a loop to create a hanger.

Susan DeRiso
Barrington, RI

Anne M. Cromwell-Gapp
Connecticut Valley Child Care Center
Claremont, NH

Lucky Rainbows

The luck o' the Irish will fill your classroom when your students make these three-dimensional rainbows. In advance, cut a large supply of colorful 1" x 5" paper strips. To make one rainbow, color a white construction paper copy of the rainbow pattern (page 98) with three colors of your choice; then cut it out. For the top band of color on your rainbow, count out nine matching construction paper strips. Curve each strip until the ends overlap; then glue them together. Hold the ends in place until they are firmly attached. Then glue each resulting ring to the corresponding rainbow band. Repeat with six strips for the middle row and four strips for the bottom row.

Trim a four-inch square of construction paper to resemble a pot, making it as large as possible. Glue this pot to the edge of the rainbow. Spread glue in the space between the pot and the rainbow; then cover that space with torn yellow construction paper nuggets. If desired, add some sparkle—use gold-glitter fabric paint to dab gold dust on the nuggets and to personalize each pot. Let these rainbows dry overnight; then display them on bulletin boards, doors, or wherever your little leprechauns desire!

JoEllyn Larrison
Northside Elementary
Geneseo, IL

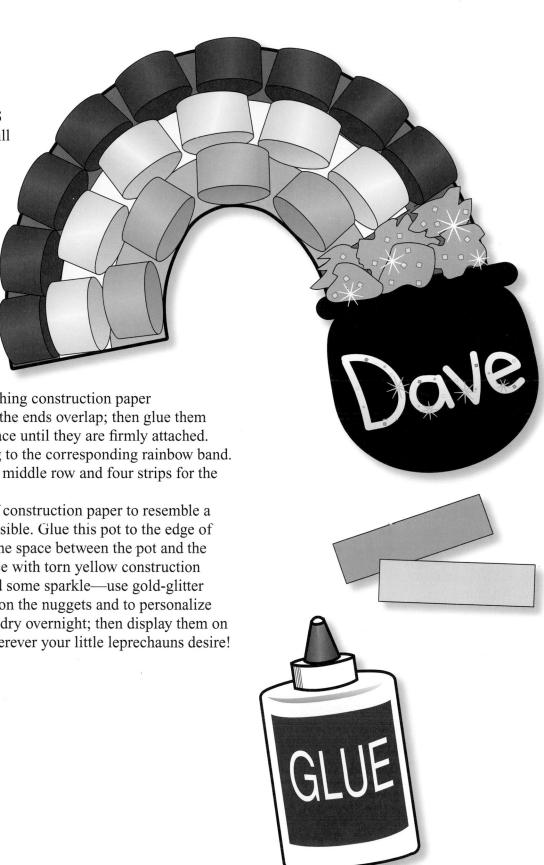

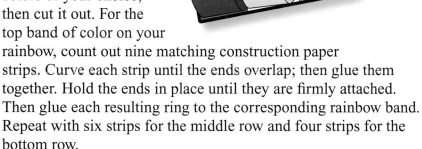

Rain, Rain, Go Away

These uplifting umbrellas will brighten up even the darkest day! Gather the materials listed below. Then help each child follow the directions. Hang the completed umbrellas from your ceiling and then batten down the hatches. The chance of rain today is 100 percent!

Materials for one:
2 paper plate halves
paint
paintbrush
construction paper
glue
colorful sticky dots (optional)
hole puncher
4 blue construction paper raindrops
blue or silver glitter
5 yarn pieces of varying lengths
scissors

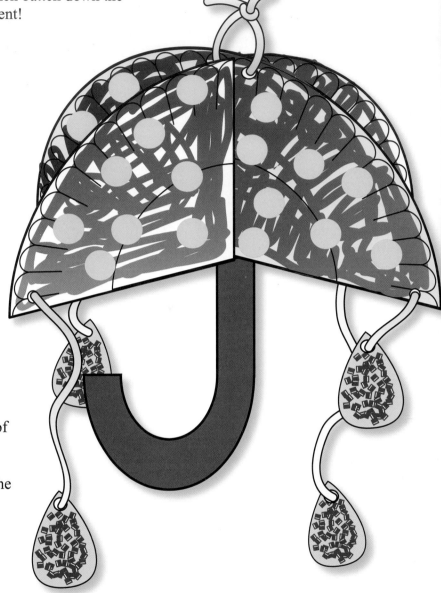

To make one:

1. Paint both sides of the paper plate halves and allow them to dry.
2. Cut a slit in one of the plate halves from the center of the straight edge to the middle of the half.
3. Cut a slit in the other plate half from the center of the curved edge to the middle of the half.
4. Cut out a construction paper handle and then glue it toward the center of one of the plate halves.
5. Slide the two plate halves together as shown.
6. Decorate the umbrella (with sticky dots if desired).
7. Apply glitter to the raindrops.
8. Punch a hole near each of the four corners of the umbrella.
9. Use a different length of yarn to tie each raindrop to the umbrella.
10. Punch two holes near the top of the umbrella; then tie the ends of the remaining yarn length to the holes to make a hanger.

Kimberli Carrier
Wise Owl Preschool
Nashua, NH

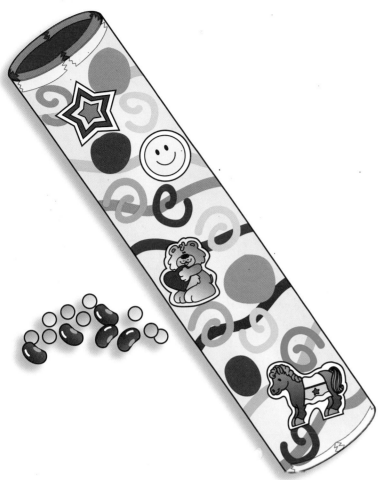

Sounds Like Rain

Tippita, tappita…Is that rain outside? No, it's this clever rain stick! To make one, cut from tagboard two circles sized to fit over the ends of a paper towel tube. Tape one circle to one end of the tube. Then decorate the tube with crayons, markers, stickers, or paint pens. Roll or crumple a large piece of aluminum foil; then twist it into a spiral shape and fit it inside the tube. (Be sure to use enough foil to reach both ends of the tube.) Pour in about a quarter cup of small dried beans, lentils, or rice. Then tape the second tagboard circle to the open end of the tube. Flip the stick from end to end to hear the sound of falling rain!

Michelle Barnea
Dover, NJ

Raindrops Falling Down on Me!

This cool art technique is sure to create oohs and aahs! In advance, tint clear Karo syrup with blue food coloring. Provide each youngster with a sheet of white construction paper. Have her draw a picture of herself either carrying an umbrella or wearing a raincoat. Next, instruct each youngster to dip a craft stick into the syrup mixture. Then have her drip small drops of the syrup on her paper to simulate raindrops. (Large drops of syrup will not harden.) After the papers are complete, allow them to dry on a flat surface for several days. The result will be shiny, wet-looking, rainy works of art!

Leanne Gibbons
Sacred Heart School
Quincy, MA

Bunny Surprise!

Youngsters will enjoy making—and especially giving—these unique springtime cards!

Materials for one:
two egg cutouts (pattern on page 99)
a stapler
Easter grass (optional)
glue
white and colored construction paper
scissors
crayons, colored pencils, or pastels
markers

To make one:
1. Decorate one of the eggs. Then, beginning at the narrower end, cut a slit partway down that egg.
2. Place the decorated egg on top of the plain egg and staple them together at the wider end. Fold back the top egg; then draw and color bunny features inside.
3. Glue the back of the plain egg to a folded piece of colored construction paper so that the decorated egg is showing and the staple is at the top.
4. Add details to the outside of the card and write a spring or Easter message on the inside.

Michele Hertz
Central Islip Early Childhood Center
Central Islip, NY

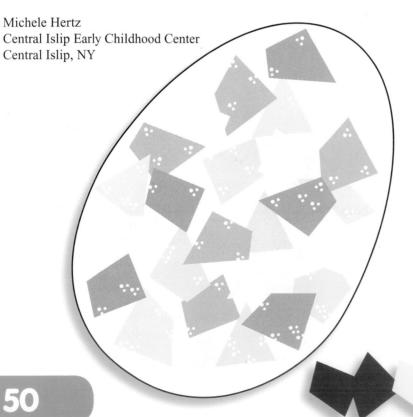

Impressive Eggs

These eggs will leave a colorful impression! Give each child an egg shape cut from white construction paper. Have her cut or tear enough small pieces of bright colors of tissue paper to cover the egg. Then have her paint white vinegar over the egg shape. Have her lay the tissue paper pieces on top of the egg, painting more vinegar over each one. When the egg is covered with colorful tissue, leave it to dry. When dry, the tissue paper pieces will fall right off, leaving behind a pretty design.

Leanne Gibbons
Sacred Heart School
Quincy, MA

Bunny Bookmarks

These bookmarks will motivate kids to hop from one book into the next! Gather the materials listed below. Then have each child cut out a bunny's head, ears, paws, and tail from white felt. Instruct the child to glue the garbage bag ties onto the backs of the bunny ears so that one end of each tie is at the tip of each ear. Help the child glue the other ends of the ties to the back of the bunny's head so that the bottom of the ears meets the top of the head as shown. Cut off any remaining length of the ties that are visible. Have the child glue the head to one end of the ribbon, the front paws below the head, and the back paws to the bottom. Next, encourage the child to add the bunny's facial features. When the glue is dry, have the child complete the bunny by gluing its tail to the back of the ribbon. Quick! Let's find a book to read!

Materials for one:
6" length of ribbon
two 10 mm wiggle-eye stickers
three 1½" pieces of thin yarn (whiskers)
scissors (decorative cut, optional)

white felt
one 8 mm pink sequin
   or pom-pom (nose)
2 white garbage bag ties
craft glue

Julie A. Koczur
Homeschool
Fort Benton, MT

Funny Bunny

These cute bunnies will be sure to step into your classroom! To begin, a child glues the rim of a white paper plate to the bottom half of a 12" x 18" sheet of dark construction paper. He glues on a pom-pom nose, pipe cleaner whiskers, and two big wiggle eyes. Next, have the child take off his shoes and socks. Paint the bottoms of both his feet with white tempera paint; then have him make two footprints above the paper plate. When the paint has dried, use a white crayon to make bunny-ear outlines around the footprints. Attach to each bunny a copy of the poem shown; then send the projects home for parents to enjoy!

Diane Bonica
Deer Creek School
Tigard, OR

This little bunny will last for years.
He is so cute, with foot-long ears!

Bunny Hats

The bunny hop will be a necessary activity after your youngsters make these adorable headbands! For each child, program a pastel sheet of construction paper as shown. Have each child cut along the black lines. Then instruct her to draw a bunny face below the ears. Have each child glue a half-inch pom-pom to the face for a nose. Then attach each bunny to a narrow strip of paper and staple each resulting headband to fit the appropriate child. Hippity hop, bunnies are on their way!

Diane Bonica
Deer Creek School
Tigard, OR

Oatmeal Bunnies

Invite youngsters to hop on over to your art table to make these Easter baskets from oatmeal canisters! Prepare the canisters by peeling off the labels and cutting a large oval on one side of each canister. Have a child paint an entire canister with tan, white, or gray tempera paint. When the paint is dry, have her glue a cotton ball tail on one end and paper ears and eyes, a pink pom-pom nose, and some pipe cleaner whiskers on the other end as shown. Stuff some Easter grass into the opening; then add Easter treats and colored eggs to this cute bunny!

Cindi Zsittnik
Hanover, MD

Easter "Bag-sket"

Invite your little bunnies to hop on over to make these Easter baskets from brown paper grocery bags! In advance, collect a class supply of grocery bags. Trim each bag to six inches above the bottom fold line. Next, cut three inches down each corner and fold each side over to make four flaps. Cut a two-inch-wide strip from the remainder (top) of the bag. Twist the strip; then staple it to the bag to make a handle as shown. Then gather the materials listed below and help each child complete the directions to finish this special Easter basket.

Materials for one:
grocery bag basket
shallow pan containing brown tempera paint
shallow pan containing green tempera paint
paintbrushes
scissors

To make one:
1. Paint a brown basket weave design around all four sides of the bag below the flaps.
2. Paint the flaps green.
3. When the paint is dry, cut the green flaps into narrow strips to resemble grass.

Carol Bruckner, Oaklawn Elementary
Fort Worth, TX

Ducky Little Baskets

Get your ducks in a row with these nifty Easter baskets. To prepare, collect a class supply of gallon-sized yellow milk jugs. (If possible, check with a local dairy for donations.) Cut the top half of each jug as shown. Provide each student with a jug. Have her glue on construction paper eyes, wings, and a beak. (If desired, glue on some yellow craft feathers, too.) Fill the basket with Easter grass, chocolate eggs, and other yummy treats. Or invite the child to use her basket on your class egg hunt. Quack, quack! Easter's on its way!

Connie Ellington
County Line Elementary
Winder, GA

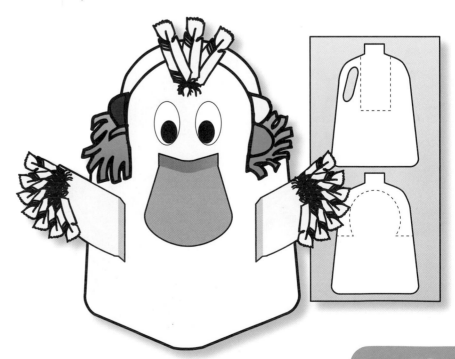

Earth Day Painting

Celebrate Earth Day with these easy-to-make paintings of our world! Have a child spoon a little green, white, and blue tempera paint onto a white construction paper circle. Then have her fold the circle in half and press from the fold outward. Have her unfold the paper and observe the beautiful mix of blue, green, and white that resembles our planet!

Laura Dickerson
Seawell Elementary
Chapel Hill, NC

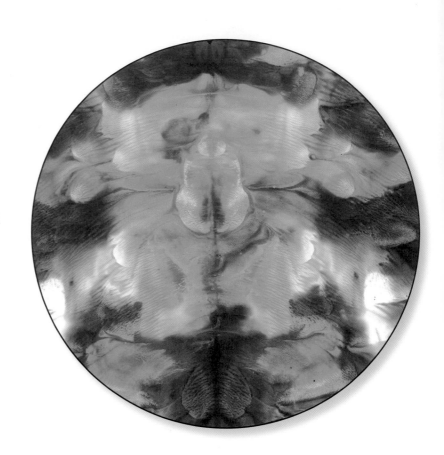

Fiesta Favors

These colorful crafts add festive flair to your Cinco de Mayo celebrations. To make one, first cut out the center of a nine-inch paper plate. Repeat with a second plate; then discard the cutouts. Cut several different colors of crepe paper streamers into 7½-inch lengths. On the front of one plate, squeeze a thin line of glue along the rim, then crisscross the streamers over the opening until it is completely covered. Glue the back of the second plate on top of the first one to frame the streamers. When the glue is dry, use markers to decorate the rim. Punch holes around the rim; then loop short lengths of colorful yarn through each hole. Wave these festive favors in a parade or classroom celebration. Olé!

Mary E. Maurer
Children's Corner Daycare
Durant, OK

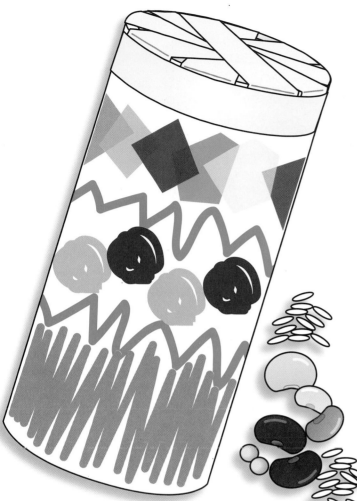

Juice Can Maracas

Celebrate Cinco de Mayo and shake things up with these fun maracas! Ask parents to help you save frozen-juice cans and their lids. When you have a class supply, have each child decorate a 4½" x 9" piece of white construction paper with colorful markers or scraps of tissue paper. Glue the paper around a can; then partially fill it with rice, dried beans, dried lentils, or pea gravel. Use colorful masking tape to securely attach the lid to the can. Then play the maracas to music with a Mexican beat!

Carla Houchin
Davis Elementary
College Place, WA

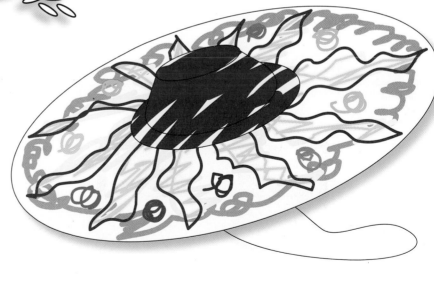

Sombreros

The beautiful colors on these sombreros are fashioned entirely by your students. To make a sombrero, cut out a 16-inch circle from poster board. Center an upside-down paper bowl on the circle; then trace around it. Cut out a hole from the poster board approximately one-half inch smaller than the traced circle. Then glue the inverted bowl around the hole. When the glue dries, staple on a length of elastic for a chin strap. Then use brightly colored paints and markers to decorate the hat. Olé!

Martie Eernisse
Cincinnati Christian School
Fairfield, OH

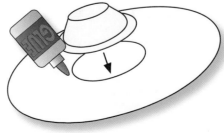

Garden in a Jar

Encourage your little ones to "plant" these everlasting gardens to give to their moms on Mother's Day. In advance, collect a small plastic jar with a lid for each child. Help the child roll out a thick layer of green play dough. Then have her use the jar lid to cut out a circle of the play dough. Have her poke a few small artificial flowers into the dough to create a unique miniature garden. Allow the dough to harden completely before gluing it to the inside of the jar lid. Screw the jar over the flowers; then attach a pretty ribbon and a copy of the poem on page 100.

Dawn Anderson
Marietta, GA

I made this gift, Mom,
Just for you,
Because you're special
And I love you, too!
No need to water it,
For it can't grow.
It's just something
To let you know...
I'm thinking of you
On your special day!

Happy Mother's Day!

Mother's Day Sachet

Moms and special ladies everywhere deserve a treat on their special day, so make these sachets that smell as good as they look! To make one sachet, run a thin bead of glue all the way around the edge of a paper doily. Sandwich a folded fabric-softener dryer sheet between this doily and an identical one. Allow the glue to dry. Using a bobby pin as a child-safe needle, sew a length of narrow ribbon around the edges of the doilies to create a decorative effect. Tie a knot in the ribbon; then use the ribbon ends to make a loop for hanging. Add a personal touch by making a thumbprint flower on one side of the sachet. Encourage children to give their sweet-smelling sachets to the special ladies in their lives.

Judy Kuen
Lomira Elementary
Lomira, WI

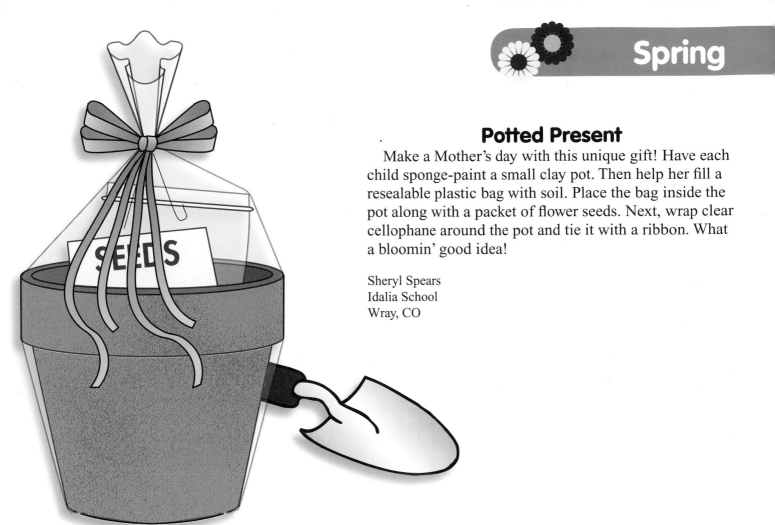

Potted Present

Make a Mother's day with this unique gift! Have each child sponge-paint a small clay pot. Then help her fill a resealable plastic bag with soil. Place the bag inside the pot along with a packet of flower seeds. Next, wrap clear cellophane around the pot and tie it with a ribbon. What a bloomin' good idea!

Sheryl Spears
Idalia School
Wray, CO

Father's Day Bookmarks

These bookmarks will give dads something to smile about for a long time to come! To make a bookmark, glue a child's photo to one end of a bordered nametag. Have the child copy the provided saying below her picture. Next, instruct her to personalize the back of the nametag and write the year. Then laminate the bookmarks and present them to all your students' proud papas!

Stephanie Feldman
Budd Lake, NJ

Let my happy face save your reading place!

Love, Kelly

2007

Hurry-Scurry Hummingbirds

Are you studying birds this spring? These child-made projects will help familiarize youngsters with one of the tiniest and fastest-flapping birds of all. In advance, display color illustrations of hummingbirds. To make one hummingbird, cut out a white construction paper copy of the hummingbird body (page 100). Use a pencil to draw on eyes and a beak. Using a thin watercolor wash, lightly paint three paper cupcake liners and the body. When the liners are dry, fold two in half for wings; then fold the remaining liner into quarters for the tail. Assemble and glue the hummingbird on a sheet of construction paper. Create an aviary effect with a display of these birds around your classroom.

Johanna Clinton
Rosemont Elementary
Dallas, TX

How "Tweet"!

These feathered friends are a perfect springtime project! First, have a child cut a zigzag line along the top of a brown or white paper lunch bag. Ask her to stuff some shredded newspaper into the bottom of the bag; then have her wrap a pipe cleaner around the bag about four inches from the top and twist it to hold the bag closed. Help her fold down the cut edge of the bag. Then have her paint the bag as she desires. Next, hot-glue a satin Christmas ball to the top of the bag (where the folded edge is). Have the child cut out a beak from orange construction paper and punch out two black paper dots for eyes. Hot-glue these to the bird's face; then hot-glue a craft feather to the back of the head so that it sticks up as shown. Have the child place the finished bird in a grapevine wreath nest.

Jane Conner
Falmouth Elementary
Falmouth, VA

"Scent-sational" Butterflies

A swarm of pretty-smelling butterflies is about to flutter into your classroom! Copy the butterfly pattern (page 101) on colorful tagboard to make a class set. Give each student a copy of the pattern and have him cut it out. Instruct him to color the butterfly body and draw a face. Have each child apply a generous amount of glue to each wing and then spread it with his finger. Next, have him add pieces of colorful potpourri to each wing. Allow the glue to dry and then hang each butterfly from the ceiling. Smells lovely!

Caroline Gartlan
Shanklin Elementary
Burton, SC

Beautiful Butterflies

Spring into spring with these beautiful butterflies. To prepare, make a class supply of the butterfly pattern (page 102) and then cut each of them out. Stock an area with the following items: butterfly cutouts, a shallow pan of water, spring-type clothespins, and crumpled tissue paper squares in a variety of colors.

To make a butterfly, have each child use a clothespin to hold a piece of tissue paper as shown. Direct him to lightly dip the paper into the water and then press the paper onto a butterfly. The tissue paper's color will bleed onto the butterfly. (Some types of tissue paper will not bleed as much as others. Be sure to test the tissue paper first.) Encourage the child to use this procedure to paint his butterfly a variety of colors. Display these masterpieces in your room or in a hallway and invite visitors to flutter by the butterflies!

Jean Gomes
M. Carey School
Waverly, IA

Fabulous Flower Carts

What's the scoop on spring? Laundry scoop flower carts! To prepare, collect a class supply of clean laundry scoops. Poke a hole in opposite sides of each one as shown. Next cut out two sturdy cardboard wheels for each scoop.

To make one flower cart, have a child use a marker to draw lines on each wheel as shown. Then help him use a brad to attach each wheel to a hole in the scoop. Have the child place a small block of Styrofoam in the scoop and then cover the Styrofoam with Easter grass. Next have him cut out small construction paper flowers and glue each one onto a toothpick. If desired, invite the child to squeeze a dot of green glue in the center of each flower. When the glue is dry, have the child gently insert each toothpick into the Styrofoam. Now that's a crafty cart!

Faye Barker and Debbie Monk
Bethesda Elementary
Durham, NC

Picket Fences and Flowers

This idea has your budding artists painting a picket masterpiece! To prepare, make several picket fence stencils by gluing together craft sticks as shown. When the glue is dry, place the stencils at a center along with the following: small sponges, flower-shaped sponges, large sheets of white construction paper, and shallow pans of green, pink, yellow, and purple paint.

To make a picket painting, have a child place fence stencils across the bottom half of his paper. Direct him to dip a small sponge into green paint and stencil around and through the fence. Next have the child use flower-shaped sponges to make pink, yellow, and purple flower prints above the fence. When the paint is dry, invite the child to add a yarn stem and construction paper leaves to each flower. Lovely!

Susan DeRiso
Barrington, RI

"Scent-sational" Painting

Your budding artists will be eager to complete these lovely smelling works of art! Have each youngster paint red flowers or hearts on a sheet of white construction paper. Before the paint dries, have the child sprinkle sugar-free strawberry gelatin powder on the wet paint. Then help her shake the excess from her paper. If desired, have each student add more details to her painting using a different color of paint. Then instruct her to sprinkle a different flavor of sugar-free gelatin over the newly painted area. Ahhh—art that's beautiful to the eyes and the nose!

Pretty Pansies

To make a pansy, use a permanent marker to draw a pansy outline on a sheet of waxed paper. Spray the waxed paper with heavy-strength spray starch. Then arrange colorful tissue paper squares on the waxed paper, overlapping them so that they cover the entire pattern. Spray on another coat of starch and then add another layer of tissue paper squares. Spray the flower one more time; then let it dry (for several hours). When the flower is completely dry, turn the waxed paper over and trim around the outline with scissors. Now remove the waxed paper backing. If desired, use a marker to draw petal outlines on the flower and then add a few construction paper leaves before displaying these colorful beauties in a sunny window.

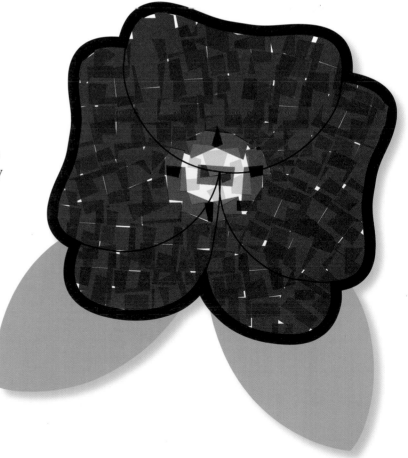

Suzanne DeVries
Evergreen Elementary
Plainfield, NJ

Height and Hands

Height and hands are the major components of these child-size sunflowers.

Materials for one:
1 margarine-tub lid (for tracing)
1 sheet of art paper per child
yellow tempera paint mixed
    with dishwashing liquid
    (or washable yellow paint)
brown tempera paint
paintbrushes
sunflower seeds
green bulletin board paper
green construction paper
1 tape measure or yardstick
glue
scissors

To begin, help a child trace the lid on a sheet of art paper. Then instruct her to paint one of her hands with the yellow paint. Have her make yellow handprints around the edge of the traced circle. After she rinses her hands, instruct the child to paint the inside of the circle brown. When the paint dries, invite the child to glue sunflower seeds to the center. When the glue is dry, have the child cut out her flower. Next measure the child from toe to shoulder. Cut out a bulletin board paper stem of that height. Have the child cut out two large construction paper leaves, then glue the stem and leaves to the flower. Mount all of these child-size flowers on a classroom wall.

Judy Kelley
Lilja School
Natick, MA

Sunflower Mosaics

This sunny sunflower project provides fabulous fine-motor practice and offers lots of opportunities for children to plan designs. To prepare, stock your art area with sturdy art paper, yellow and green construction paper, glue, and dried beans. Encourage each child to tear the yellow and green construction paper, then arrange and glue the pieces on the art paper to make a sunflower picture. Then have him glue the dried beans to the center. (This is one time when a lot of glue will be necessary.) Encourage each child to take his sunflower mosaic home to share with his family.

Laura Crymes
Canongate Elementary
Sharpsburg, GA

Plant Prints

This art idea integrates science and is an easy way to show youngsters the power of the pigment chlorophyll. It's one of nature's paints!

Materials for one:

various leaves from plants
blades of grass
2 sheets of newsprint paper
wooden or metal spoon
tape

rolling pin
folded construction paper card
glue stick
insect stickers

To make one:

1. Place a sheet of newsprint on a tabletop or other smooth surface.
2. Arrange leaves and grass on the paper.
3. Cover the arrangement with the second sheet of newsprint and tape it in place.
4. Use the back of the spoon and/or the rolling pin to rub the paper (the more pressure, the better).
5. Remove the top sheet of paper and the leaves and grass pieces.
6. Trim the print to fit the card. Glue it in place and embellish with stickers.

Linda Masternak Justice
Kansas City, MO

A Handy Display

Hands down, this supersized refrigerator magnet will encourage your students to do their best work. In advance, program a sheet of paper as shown. Duplicate the page on construction paper to create a class supply. Gather the materials listed below and then follow the directions. Encourage each youngster to take his completed project home and use it all year long to show off his super work!

Materials for one:
programmed page
11" x 14" piece of poster board
marker
shallow pan containing a thin layer
    of paint
newsprint
glue stick
two 4" strips of magnetic tape

To make one:
1. Have each child write his name.
2. Help him press his hands in the paint and blot them on newsprint. Then help him make prints on his programmed page.
3. Allow the paint to dry; then glue the paper to the center of the poster board. (Laminate the project, if desired.)
4. Add four-inch strips of magnetic tape to the back of the poster board (top and bottom).

adapted from an idea by Jan Harding
Crescent Elementary
Sandy, UT

Dina Is a Superstar!

Sparkling Stars

Don't shy away from glitter—it's easy and neat with this project! For each child, cut out a star shape from construction paper. Program each star with the phrase "[Child's name] Is a Superstar!" Next, mix some glitter with clear hair gel. Invite each child to use a paintbrush to spread the glittery gel over her star. Once the gel is dry, set it with a little hairspray. Display the finished stars around your classroom door to let everyone know your class is simply heavenly!

Leslie O'Donnell
Sedalia Park School
Marietta, GA

Fingerpainted Football Jerseys

Touchdown! These child-made jerseys are sure to score big with your students! For each child, cut out a large football jersey shape from fingerpaint paper. Then use masking tape to spell each child's first or last name on a different jersey. Also tape a number of the child's choice to the jersey. To complete her jersey, have a child fingerpaint her cutout completely, covering the tape too. When the paint is dry, help each child carefully peel off the tape to reveal his name and jersey number. A winning lineup of these personalized jerseys boosts student spirit!

Angelina Vargo
Hansel and Gretel Early Learning Center
Harrisburg, PA

PERRY 10

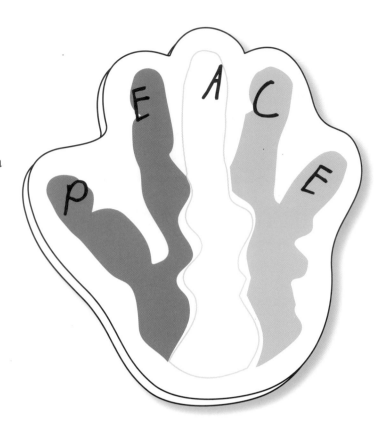

Give Peace a Hand

What's red, white, and blue and spells *peace,* too? A magnet straight from the hands of your students! To make one magnet, paint a child's right palm, thumb, and fingers with red, white, and blue tempera paint to make a striped design. Have him press his hand onto a sheet of light-colored craft foam. When the paint is dry, cut around the handprint. Then have the child use a black permanent marker to write the word *PEACE* across the fingers as shown. Add a strip of magnetic tape to the back and send these patriotic projects home to adorn family fridges!

Heather Carney
Sycamore Tree Christian Child Care Center
Hartford, WI

Star-Spangled Display

Use pasta to make this memorable flag display! In advance, create a supply of red rigatoni pasta by combining one box of rigatoni, one-eighth cup of red food coloring, and one-half cup of rubbing alcohol in a resealable plastic bag. Allow the pasta to sit for five minutes, turning the bag every minute to evenly coat the pasta. Lay the pasta on a brown paper bag and allow it to dry completely. Next, program a class supply of 8" x 10" white tagboard pieces with the American flag pattern as shown.

To begin the activity, give each child a piece of tagboard and 27 pieces of pasta. Instruct her to glue her pasta onto every other stripe on the flag as shown. Then give each child a 3" x 4" piece of blue construction paper and 13 silver star stickers. Explain to the class that the first American flag had 13 stars on it to represent the 13 colonies. Direct each child to place her star stickers on her construction paper piece and then glue it in the upper left corner of the flag. Display the flags on a bulletin board with the title "Hooray for the Red, White, and Blue!"

Ann Schmidt
Lafayette Christian School
Lafayette, IN

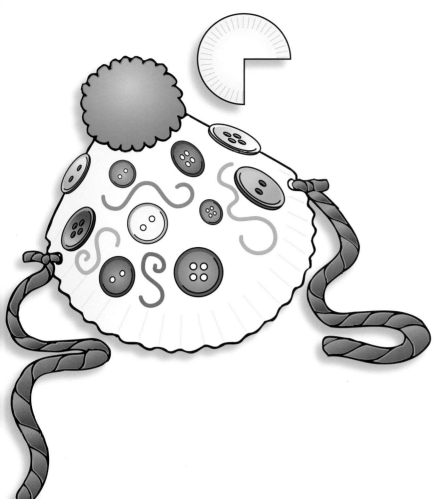

Let's Celebrate!

No matter what the celebration, these easy-to-make party hats are a perfect fit. To prepare, gather an assortment of craft items, glue, a stapler, and a hole puncher. Each child will also need a nine-inch paper plate, two 20-inch pieces of yarn, and a large pom-pom. Cut out one-fourth of each plate, as shown. Next, overlap and staple together the cut edges of the plate to form a cone-shaped hat. Have each child decorate her hat. Then punch a hole on each side of the hat and help the child tie a piece of yarn to each hole. To finish the hat, invite the child to glue the large pom-pom to its point.

Lin Attaya
Hodge Elementary
Denton, TX

Recycled Bookmarks

Doing a unit on the post office? Bet you'll have lots of leftover stamps! Here's a great way to put them to use. Cut a 5" x 2" strip of colored construction paper for each child. Have the child glue three canceled stamps to one side of the strip. Laminate the strips and cut them out. At a second sitting, have the child punch a hole near one end of his strip and then loop several colorful strands of yarn through the hole. Presto—a well-traveled bookmark! If desired, have each student make several of these bookmarks to have extras on hand to give to parents and other classroom volunteers.

Bernadean Clothier
Neithercut-Flint Community Schools
Flint, MI

Sunglasses Pouch

Sunglasses rarely come with their own cases, so why not have your students create these pouches as gifts? Duplicate the sunglasses greeting (page 103) on colored tagboard for each child. Each child also needs a seven-inch square of craft foam, access to a hole puncher, two pipe cleaners, fabric paints, glue, and sequins. To make a pouch, fold the foam square in half. Through both thicknesses, punch holes that are approximately an inch apart along one end and the open side as shown. Use pipe cleaners to lace up the pouch. If there is leftover pipe cleaner, simply lace it back through to add reinforcement. Finish the pouch with a little decoration. Direct each child to cut out a sunglasses greeting, sign his name, and slide it into the pouch. Here comes the sun!

Tonya House
Anna's Little Red Schoolhouse
Bowling Green, KY

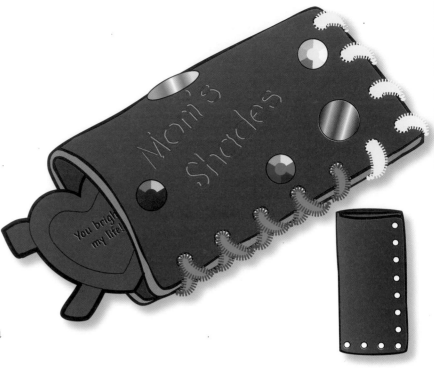

Sensational Stationery

Here's an idea for an inexpensive yet very useful gift for parents, volunteers, and student teachers—stationery designed by your students! To prepare, measure two inches down from the top of a sheet of paper and then use a marker to draw a line straight across. Copy the paper to make a class set. Give each student a copy and have him use a pencil to draw a simple picture or scene. Then trace over each drawing with a fine-tipped marker. Make five copies of each student's paper. Next, have the child color the drawing at the top of each page. Fold each set of stationery to fit a business-sized envelope. To complete each gift, tie together the folded sheets and five envelopes with a length of ribbon. Ta-da!

Mary Kay Good
Lima, Peru
South America

Sweet Peas

Picture your sweet peas in these adorable frames that make excellent anytime gifts! To make one frame, glue four large craft sticks together to form a square. Paint the frame yellow; then set it aside to dry. Cut out green construction paper copies of two pea pods (page 104). To make one pod, glue only the bottoms and sides of the patterns together, forming a boat shape. When the glue is dry, tuck three or four green ½-inch pom-poms inside the pod and glue them in place. Poke a short length of green pipe cleaner through one end of the pod; then twist the pipe cleaner to look like a vine. Use a permanent marker to write "I'm Your Sweet Pea!" on the dry frame. Glue the pea pod to the bottom of the frame. After each child has made a frame, help him glue a picture of himself into it. Finally, attach magnetic tape to the back of the frame. How sweet it is!

adapted from an idea by Patricia Draper
Millarville Community School
Millarville, Alberta, Canada

For "Thumb-body" Special

Say thank you to classroom helpers with this idea for an unforgettable framed photo! To begin, write large letters to spell the words *thank you* on individual sheets of tagboard. Then take a group photo of your students holding the letters to spell the message. Make a 3" x 5" copy of the photo for each helper you wish to thank.

Make a frame for each photo gift by drawing a 3" x 5" rectangle in the center of a 5" x 7" piece of card stock. Write "You Are 'Thumb-body' Special!" on the frame as shown. Then have students add their thumbprints around the frame. Write each child's name next to her print. Then use double-sided tape to attach a copy of the photo to the center of each rectangle. Thank you!

Jessica Wells
Baker Elementary
Moorestown, NJ

Ceramics Studio

This creative center will make your little ones feel like they have their very own ceramics studio. Set up a center with plaster of paris, water, plastic cups, craft sticks (for mixing), and a variety of flexible molds, such as plaster-craft molds and candy molds. Also provide a variety of craft paints and paintbrushes. Then illustrate step-by-step directions according to the directions on your particular plaster of paris. Display these directions in the center. Supply each child with a small box or box lid for the pieces he is working on. (Also set aside space nearby for projects to dry.) After demonstrating the process, encourage each child to visit this ceramics studio during center time and create to his heart's content.

Bonnie McKenzie
Cheshire Country Day School
Cheshire, CT

Outside Art

Step outside for a bit of process art that's guaranteed to inspire the creativity of artists and observers alike! In advance, use clothespins to hang a long length of butcher paper along your schoolyard fence. Then send your children out with paints, paintbrushes, and plastic tubs of water. Explain where children can pour out dirty water and fill up with clean water. Then let the process begin. The sky's the limit—really!

Sandra Steele
Jefferson School
Princeton, IL

Colorful Spinners

Use this simple craft to create a rainbow of beautiful, spinning colors in your classroom! Give each child a paper plate and a supply of markers. Have her color the entire plate using a variety of colors. Then help each child push a brad through the center of the bottom of her plate and fasten it on top as shown. Now, encourage your little ones to spin, spin, spin their spinners!

Anne M. Cromwell-Gapp
Connecticut Valley Child Care Center
Claremont, NH

Sand-Art Scenes

Colored sand adds new dimension and texture to your youngsters' artwork. Collect six small margarine tubs with lids. Fill each tub about three-quarters full of sand. Add eight to ten drops of food coloring to each one to make a different color of sand. After securing the lids, shake the tubs until the sand is evenly colored. Then give each child a sheet of construction paper, a paintbrush, and a 4:1 mixture of glue and water. Instruct each child to use the glue to paint one part of a landscape, such as the trees, grass, or mountains. Then have him sprinkle a color of sand onto the glue and shake off the excess. Encourage the child to paint the next part of his scene, painting and sanding as before. Continue in this manner until the picture is finished. Back the sandy scenes with a complementary color for display.

Sandie Bolze
Verne W. Critz School
East Patchogue, NY

Crayon Conducting

Use this open-ended art activity to inspire your youngsters' creativity and listening skills. Play a recording of classical music while youngsters close their eyes and listen. Then discuss with students what they have heard. Explain that sometimes many different people play instruments during a piece of music, and that one person, called a conductor, directs them all. Replay the music and demonstrate how the conductor would move his baton as the music's tempo changes. Then provide each student with a large sheet of art paper and a crayon. As music plays, have each child conduct with a crayon on her paper. After a minute or so, change the music and have students trade crayons to add different colors to their drawings. Bravo!

April Sutherland
Sacred Heart School for the Arts
Mount Vernon, NY

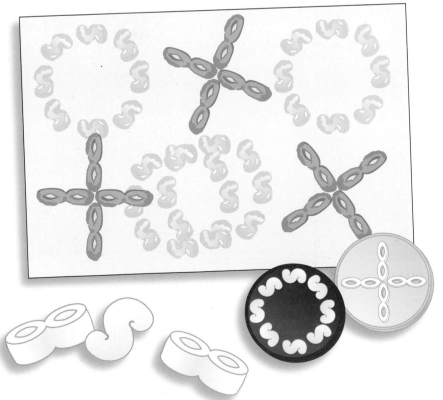

Styrofoam Stamps

Use Styrofoam packing pieces to make this unique artwork. Collect several small plastic lids. Hot-glue packing pieces randomly or in a pattern to the top of each lid. Pour paint in a shallow pan. Invite each child to dip a stamp in the paint and then use both hands to repeatedly press the stamp onto a sheet of paper to make prints. Encourage each youngster to create patterns or pictures with the stamps. Once stamping is complete, blot the stamps with a damp paper towel and store them for later use.

Julie Brown
Wake Forest, NC

Maracas

Can you hear the rhythm of the beat? The magic of these maracas is contagious! On a sheet of tagboard, draw simple illustrations and write the directions as shown. (If desired, you can just enlarge and duplicate the illustration on this page.) Then stock a center with a supply of dried beans or rice, plastic cups, masking tape, bottles of dimensional craft paint, and the directions. To make a maraca, have a child follow the directions. Encourage youngsters to shake their completed maracas to the beat of some traditional and some contemporary music.

Maurie F. Ganther
Virginia Beach, VA

1 paint
2 dry
3 10 beans
4 upside down
5 tape
6 shake

Lots o' Dots

Introduce your young artists to the technique of *pointillism*—painting with dots of color instead of brushstrokes. Set out various colors of tempera paint in shallow containers. Then have students use your choice of instruments to dip into the paint and make dots on their papers. You might try cotton swabs, pencil eraser tips, or fingertips. Or make giant pointillism works of art with large sheets of paper and bingo daubers in a variety of colors. Either way, encourage students to make individual dots close together to form lines and to fill in areas. The results will be pointedly pretty!

Daphne M. Orenshein
Yavneh Hebrew Academy
Los Angeles, CA

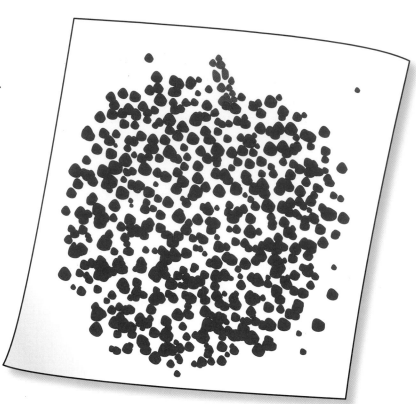

Salt in Sequence

Admirers will be layering on the compliments when they see this beautiful salt art! To prepare, gather a clean baby food jar with a lid for each child. Next, mix powdered tempera paint with table salt to create several different colors of salt. To make a jar of salt art, each child should choose two colors of salt. Have her spoon a layer of colored salt into her jar. Then instruct her to spoon a layer of her other chosen salt color into her jar. Have her repeat this process until she has filled the jar with alternating layers. Add the lid and this patterned project is complete.

Antonio Kling
Haw Creek Elementary
Asheville, NC

Shapely Clowns

Bring in these clowns to reinforce shapes and body parts! Put your children's silly clown creations on a bulletin board parade; then encourage each child to identify the clowns' shapes and body parts. It's the greatest display on earth!

Materials for one:

white construction paper
a variety of large colorful sheets
   of construction paper
one 11" circle tracer
large basic shape tracers
scissors

glue
yarn
bingo markers
assorted markers
1 large pom-pom

Teacher preparation for one:

1. Trace and cut out an 11-inch, white construction paper circle.
2. Trace a large basic shape on colorful construction paper. (If abilities permit, have your students do these steps for themselves.)

To make a clown, give a child a white construction paper circle for the clown's head. Then invite him to cut out a large (pretraced) shape and glue it to his clown's head to resemble a funny body. Next, help him trace his hands and feet onto colorful construction paper, cut them out, and then glue them to the clown's body. After adding a pom-pom nose, encourage the child to use the art supplies to create additional facial features, a hat, and decorations for his clown's costume.

Carolyn Schroeder and Mary Jones
South Terrace Elementary
Carlton, MN

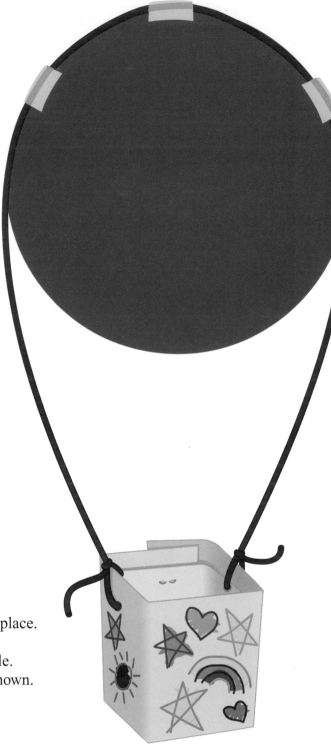

Hot-Air Balloons

To prepare, gather and clean a class supply of individual-serving milk cartons. Measure three inches up from the bottom of each carton; then cut off and discard the remaining portion. Gather the materials listed below and then guide each child to follow the directions to make her own hot-air balloon.

Materials for one:
individual-serving milk carton (cleaned, dried, and trimmed)
3" x 11" construction paper strip
large construction paper circle
stickers, markers, and crayons
stapler
hole puncher
1 length of yarn
tape

To make one:
1. Use stickers, markers, and crayons to decorate the construction paper strip.
2. Wrap the strip around the milk carton and staple it into place.
3. Hole-punch opposite sides of the milk carton.
4. Attach the middle of a yarn length to the top of the circle.
5. Tie the ends of the yarn to either side of the carton as shown. Tape the yarn in place.
6. Hang to display.

Brenda Hume
Sangaree Elementary
Summerville, SC

Pirate Kent

staple

Hello There, Matey!

Wouldn't your young pirates just love to have parrots of their own to perch on their shoulders? They can when they make these cute paper parrots and hats! To make a hat, cut two 6" x 18" pieces of black construction paper in a simple pirate hat shape as shown. Staple the pieces together four inches or more from each end where indicated. Use a white crayon to label each hat with a different child's name. Make simple patterns for a parrot's head, wings, beak, and feet from tagboard, using the illustration as a guide. To make a parrot, fold a 2½" x 12" strip of construction paper into a triangle and staple the overlapping edges as shown. Next, use the patterns to trace and cut out the parrot's features from appropriate colors of construction paper. Glue the parts together and draw two large eyes. Then have each youngster put on his hat and perch his paper parrot on his shoulder, using a long strip of masking tape to hold it in place. Squawk!

Diane Bonica
Deer Creek School
Tigard, OR

Tropical Feathered Friend

Put little hands to work to create this perky parrot! To prepare, make a class set of tagboard copies of the parrot pattern on page 105. Cut a large supply of colorful tissue paper strips. Instruct each child to cut out his parrot pattern. Then have him color both sides of the parrot, adding an eye to the back side of the pattern. Instruct each youngster to cut on the dotted lines to create wing and tail-feather openings. Next, help each child thread tissue paper strips into the openings, as shown, to create wings and tail feathers. Finally, punch a hole near the top of the parrot and add a loop of yarn for hanging. Polly want a cracker?

Cindy Richey
Weber-Hardin Elementary
Mathis, TX

A Merry Carousel

These festive projects take a little time, but the results are well worth it! Are you ready to ride?

Materials for one:
copies of the carousel ponies on page 106
two 7" paper plates
two 7" to 10" circular doilies (plain or child decorated)
10 pipe cleaners (assorted colors)
five 1" sections of toilet paper tubes
hole puncher
glue
scissors
crayons

To make one:
1. Color the carousel ponies. Cut out the colored ponies and set them aside.
2. Stack the two plates; then punch five equidistant holes through both thicknesses (as shown).
3. To make a carousel pole, twist two pipe cleaners together; then poke one end of the twisted pair through a hole in one paper plate. Spread apart the pipe cleaner tips to keep the plate from sliding off. Repeat this process for each of the five holes in that plate.
4. Glue one pony to each ring; then slip each ring over a different carousel pole.
5. To add the top canopy, slide the free end of each pole through a hole in the second paper plate and spread apart the pipe cleaner ends.
6. Glue a doily to the top and bottom plates as shown.

Display these very merry carousels on a classroom counter. Or poke a hole in the center of the top plate; insert and knot a length of curling ribbon to make a hanger; then suspend each project.

adapted from an idea by Tracey Jean Quezada
Presentation of Mary Academy
Hudson, NH

Step 2

Step 3

Step 4

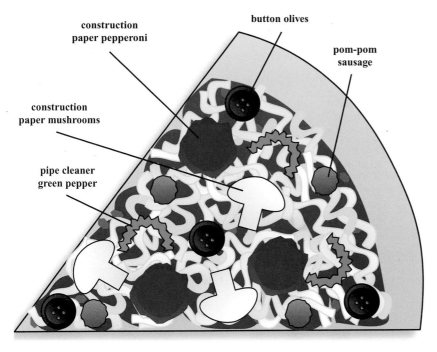

construction paper pepperoni

button olives

pom-pom sausage

construction paper mushrooms

pipe cleaner green pepper

Pizza Pizzazz

Spice up your art activities with this personal pizza project. In advance, cut out a cardboard or tagboard pizza slice for each child. To make one slice of pizza, paint red pizza "sauce" on the slice. While the paint is still wet, sprinkle on dried oregano, and then lightly press on shredded tissue paper to resemble cheese. When the paint is dry, glue on your choice of creative toppings (see the illustration for ideas). If desired, glue each personal pizza piece onto a different paper plate. Then display all the plates on a red-and-white checked background titled "Pizza Pizzazz!" Mmmm—it's positively pizza!

Janeen Danielsen
Dike Discovery Center
Dike, IA

Hey Diddle Diddle!

Reinforce the nursery rhyme and practice fine-motor skills by making these cows that really are airborne! Give each child a paper plate, a cow pattern (page 107), and a pipe cleaner. You'll also need to provide access to gray or silver paint, small sponges, scissors, glue (or tape), and crayons. To make this project, have each child sponge-paint his plate to resemble the moon. While the paint dries, instruct the child to color and cut out the cow. Have the child finish the craft by gluing (or taping) one end of the pipe cleaner to the back of the moon and the other end to the back of the cow. Jump, cow, jump!

Trish Davis
Poplarville Lower Elementary
Poplarville, MS

Dinosaur Prints

Giggles and grins abound when these crafty creatures go on display. And *you'll* know the load of learning that took place in the process! To begin, paint the bottom of a child's foot with his choice of a washable paint color. Then have him make a footprint on a sheet of construction paper. After he's washed his foot, give him an assortment of markers and craft supplies; then invite him to transform his footprint into a prehistoric creature. When the artist is through, help him name his work of art, somehow incorporating his own name. When all the projects are displayed, read all the made-up names together. You might even like to surprise your class with a previously made "[Ms. MacGregor]-osaurus"!

Nancy MacGregor
Spring Glen Elementary
Hamden, CT

Tips for Making a *T. rex*

Here's a creative way to make dinosaur skeletons using cotton swabs. To prepare, duplicate the *Tyrannosaurus rex* outline pattern on page 108 onto tagboard a few times; then cut out the patterns to make tagboard tracers. Duplicate the skull shape onto white copy paper to make a class supply. Then cut a supply of cotton swabs into halves and fourths, and have some full-length cotton swabs available too.

To make a skeleton, a child uses a white crayon to trace a *T. rex* outline onto black construction paper. Then he glues various lengths of cotton swabs over the pattern, outlining the bones. Help him use a hole puncher to punch out the nostrils and eye of the skull pattern where indicated; then have him glue the skull in place on the pattern. "Dino-mite!"

Marcia Murphy
Children's Learning Center at North Kansas City Hospital
North Kansas City, MO

Piggy Banks

Use milk jugs to make these curly-tailed cuties for holding students' pennies! In advance, collect a clean, gallon-size milk or water jug with a lid for each child. For each bank, have a child cut out two triangle ears and a circle snout from pink construction paper and then glue them in place, as shown, with the snout on the jug lid. Have her add two sticky-dot eyes. Next, have her glue four clean plastic condiment cups to the bottom of the jug to form feet. Instruct her to curl a pink pipe cleaner around her finger and then tape one end of the tail to the back of the pig. Finally, have an adult cut a slit in the top of the bank for dropping in coins. Encourage each child to take her bank home to hold her savings. When she wants to dip into her savings, she simply pops off the jug lid to retrieve the money!

Barb Miles
Charles A. Upson Elementary
Lockport, NY

Monkey Mural

Excitement builds when youngsters see the work of famous Chinese painter Wang Yani as you share the book *A Young Painter: The Life and Paintings of Wang Yani—China's Extraordinary Young Artist* by Zheng Zhensun and Alice Low. After sharing her paintings of monkeys (done when she was close to the age of your students), invite your youngsters to paint a monkey mural of their own! Provide gray, black, brown, and white tempera paint and a long length of white bulletin board paper. Review Wang Yani's monkey paintings, then watch as your inspired young painters create!

Donna Hammond, Newport Elementary, Newport, ME

Ant Art

Youngsters will scurry on over to your art center to create these ant farms! To make one, have a child paint the bottom three-fourths of a sheet of brown tagboard or cardstock with diluted glue. Have him sprinkle sand over the glue and then shake off the excess. While the glue is still wet, show him how to use a finger to draw tunnels and passageways in the sand. Then have him glue on a few black paper shapes to represent busy ants inside the farm. Finish the project by writing "[Child's name]'s Ant Farm" at the top. Allow the glue to dry thoroughly before displaying this awesome ant artwork!

Dig Deeper

Use this art activity to follow up a reading of Claude Delafosse and Gallimard Jeunesse's *Under the Ground: Hidden World* or any book about animals that live underground. Simply direct each child to use crayons to draw and color on a sheet of white paper a variety of animals she might see below the ground. (Hint to your students that the heavier the crayon mark, the better the picture will turn out.) When the drawings are complete, provide brown watercolor paint for each child to use in painting a thin, watery wash over her drawing to resemble the underground soil. Mount these illustrations side by side on a bulletin board for a huge underground display. If desired, add in some writing practice by having students label each object found in the display.

Jennifer Barton
Elizabeth Green School
Newington, CT

Hedgie's Hat

Follow up a reading of Jan Brett's *The Hat* (G. P. Putnam's Sons) with this cute craft. Gather the materials listed below. To make a hedgehog, color the center portions of the paper plate halves and a small part of the larger plate's rim brown as shown. Then color the rest of the plates' rims black. Cut slits along the black rims to resemble prickles. Glue the small plate to the larger plate, aligning the cut edges. Then attach a wiggle-eye sticker and glue a pom-pom nose to the brown part of the outer rim.

To make the sock hat, simply cut a sock shape from red paper and use sponge shapes and white paint to print a design on it. Finish the project by stapling the hat onto Hedgie's head. Use the hedgehogs to decorate a wall, or display them together with children's writing about the story.

Materials for one:

one 9" paper plate half
one 6" paper plate half
black and brown crayons
one 15 mm wiggle-eye sticker
1 black pom-pom
1 sheet of red construction paper

sponge shapes
white tempera paint
glue
scissors
access to a stapler

Helaine Donnelly and Angela Potzer
Washington School
Plainfield, NJ

Masked Bandits

Who are those masked critters? Raccoons, of course! To make one, cut off the top two inches of a brown paper lunch bag. Have each child glue a black construction paper mask shape onto the folded bottom of his bag; then instruct him to cut out circles from both white and black paper and glue them to the mask to make eyes. Next, have each child use a white crayon to trace four hand shapes onto black construction paper. Then have him cut out the shapes and glue them to the bag to represent the raccoon's feet. Instruct him to cut two ears and a nose from brown construction paper. Finally, have him use a black marker to draw stripes and a mouth on the raccoon's body as shown.

Kathleen Rose
Park Falls Elementary
Park Falls, WI

Corn Syrup Chameleon

After sharing Eric Carle's *The Mixed-Up Chameleon*, encourage your youngsters to make colorful chameleons of their own! In advance, duplicate the chameleon pattern on page 109 onto tagboard to make a class supply. Have each child cut out his pattern. Then mix containers of light corn syrup with various colors of food coloring. Have each young artist dip a finger into the corn syrup paint and fingerpaint his chameleon. Have him add other colors as he desires. Allow the paint to dry thoroughly before displaying these lovely lizards! (Factors such as humidity will affect drying time.)

Leanne Gibbons
Sacred Heart School
Quincy, MA

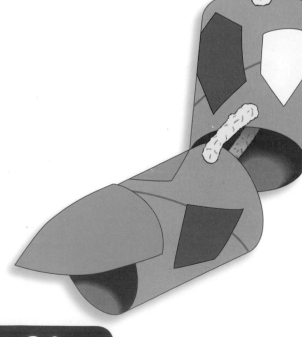

S-s-super Snake

This colorful snake is totally tubular! In advance, enlist the help of parents in collecting three toilet paper tubes for each child. To make a snake, punch holes in the ends of the tubes and then thread short pieces of pipe cleaner through the holes, twisting them to secure. Have each youngster cut out from construction paper a snake's head and tail similar to the ones shown. Instruct him to draw eyes and glue a red tongue to the head. Then have him glue the head and tail to opposite ends of the body. To finish, instruct him to glue scraps of construction paper to his snake for decoration. Hiss!

Suzanne Giaimo
Bryant Elementary
Milwaukee, WI

Artsy Alligators

These tongue-depressor alligators are sure to make little ones open up and say "Aah!" Gather the materials listed below and then help each child follow the directions. Use the finished gators as counters, as nonstandard units of measurement, or as figures for habitats.

Materials for one:
— two large craft sticks
— two 5" green pipe cleaners
— craft glue
— uncooked rice
— green tempera paint
— paintbrush
— two 7 mm wiggle-eye stickers

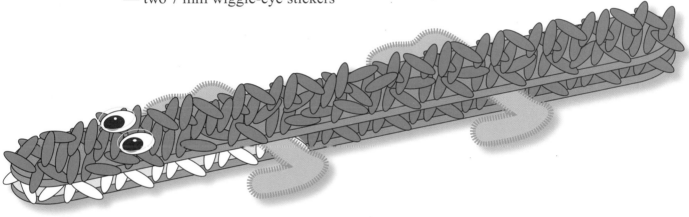

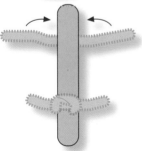

To make one:

1. Wrap and twist the pipe cleaner pieces around one of the craft sticks to form legs as shown.
2. Glue the two craft sticks together to form the alligator's body.
3. Spread glue on the top side of the body. Cover the glue with a layer of rice. Then squirt glue along the open edges between the sticks and fill in the gaps with rice.
4. When the glue is dry, paint the whole alligator green, except for the rice between the sticks on one end. (This will represent the alligator's teeth.)
5. When the paint is dry, attach the wiggle-eye stickers.

Busy Spiders

A reading of Eric Carle's *The Very Busy Spider* is sure to inspire your youngsters to complete this art activity. Gather the materials below and then help each child follow the directions to complete her own very busy spider!

Materials for one:
2" green construction paper circle (head)
2" x 4" red construction paper oval (body)
glue
2 paper reinforcements (eyes)
4 black pipe cleaners (legs)
black and red markers
tape

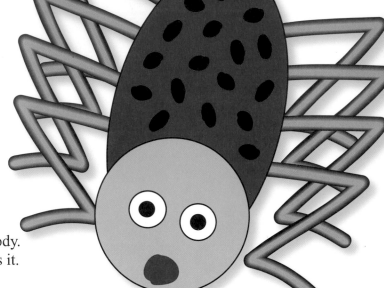

To make one:
1. Glue the head to one end of the body.
2. Attach the eyes.
3. Use the markers to add details to the face and body.
4. Turn the spider body over and lay the legs across it.
5. Tape the legs in place.
6. Bend each leg.

adapted from an idea by Sandy Blumstein
Paley Day Care Center
Philadelphia, PA

Dazzling Dragonflies

Dazzle 'em with these easy-to-make dragonflies! To make one, use markers to add eyes and some color to an old-fashioned wooden clothespin. Next tie a ten-inch length of monofilament line into a loop. Also cut two rectangles (about 5" x 8") from different colors of cellophane. Holding the clothespin with the open end up, slide the loop, then the two cellophane pieces into the clothespin. Dangle these dainty insects in front of a sunny window.

Sharon M. Coulter
Park Place Children's Center
Muncie, IN

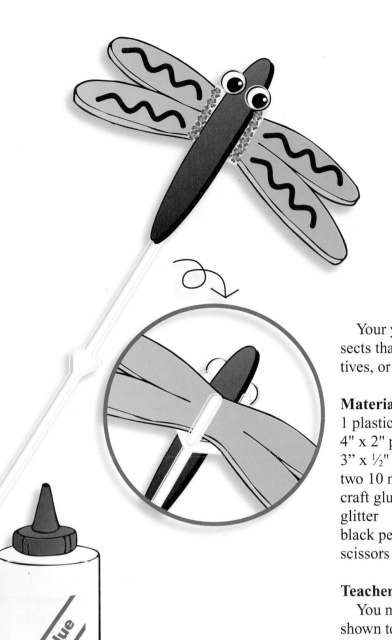

Dragonflies

Your youngsters will fly away with these crafty insects that can be used as stick puppets, math manipulatives, or individual pointers (for reading the room).

Materials for one:
1 plastic card pick (used in floral arrangements)
4" x 2" piece of colorful craft foam
3" x ½" piece of black craft foam
two 10 mm wiggle-eye stickers
craft glue
glitter
black permanent marker
scissors

Teacher preparation:
You may choose to cut the colorful craft foam as shown to resemble wings instead of having students cut it.

To make one:
1. Insert wings into the card pick as shown.
2. Trim the black craft foam into an oval body shape and glue it to the top of the pick so that it covers the middle of the wings.
3. Attach the wiggle-eye stickers. (They should cover the ends of the side prongs.)
4. Spread glue on the side prongs and apply glitter.
5. Draw a squiggly line on each wing.

Colleen Dabney
Williamsburg, VA

Lovely Ladybug Magnets

To make one ladybug, fill a plastic spoon with plaster of paris. Before the plaster sets completely, gently push in a magnet. Allow the plaster to dry overnight; then pop it out of the spoon. Use sandpaper to file any rough edges. Then paint the rounded side of the plaster to resemble a ladybug. When the paint is dry, set it with acrylic spray; then attach wiggle-eye stickers. If desired, encourage each child to give his ladybug to a special lady in his life.

Wendy Rapson
Kids in Action
Hingham, MA

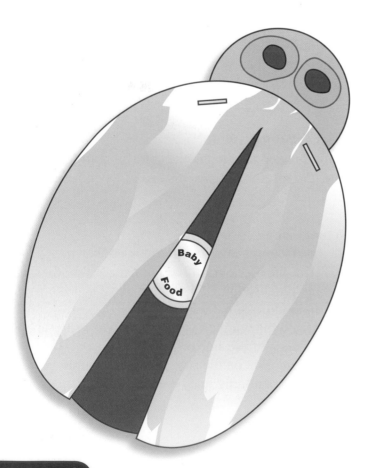

Click Beetle

After sharing Eric Carle's story *The Very Clumsy Click Beetle*, invite your young artists to make click beetles of their own. For each child, cut a body-and-head shape (about ten inches long) from white oaktag. Cut a hole 1½ inches in diameter near the center of the body. For the wings, cut an oval the same size as the beetle's body from white construction paper; then cut a slit through the center, stopping about an inch from one end. To complete the beetle, a child uses watercolors to paint the beetle's body black, the head blue, and the wings green or yellow. Hot-glue the lid of a baby food jar over the hole in the body; then staple the wings over the lid as shown. Have each child glue on green and black tissue paper circles to make the beetle's eyes. Then just have him press on the jar lid to hear his beetle click!

Lori Hosking
Milford Hill Learning Center
Milford, PA

Bees to Behold!

Youngsters will make a beeline to create these cute critters! To make one, paint the back of a small paper plate bright yellow. When the yellow paint is dry, paint on black stripes, plus a curved line for the bee's head. When the black paint is dry, glue two waxed paper wings on top of the bee's body. Then glue a black construction paper stinger to the underside of the bee's body. Complete the bee by gluing on two black construction paper eyes.

Leanne Gibbons
Sacred Heart School
Quincy, MA

Snazzy Snails

Invite your youngsters to make these cute little creatures to decorate a bulletin board or windowsill.

Materials for one:

1 small paper plate	scissors
brown and yellow tempera paint	glue
paintbrushes	red marker
1 large craft stick or wooden spoon	
one 10 mm wiggle-eye sticker	

To make one:
1. Paint the front of the paper plate brown.
2. Paint one side of the craft stick yellow.
3. After the paint dries, cut a one-inch spiral into the plate. (You may want to draw the line for the child to follow.)
4. Glue the two cut edges of the plate to cover half of the craft stick.
5. Attach the wiggle-eye sticker to the other end of the craft stick.
6. Draw on a smile.

Susan DeRiso
John W. Horton Elementary
Cranston, RI

Swimming Turtles

Invite youngsters to dive right in and create some beautiful underwater art featuring swimming turtles! Gather the materials listed below. Then help each youngster follow the directions to complete his underwater scene.

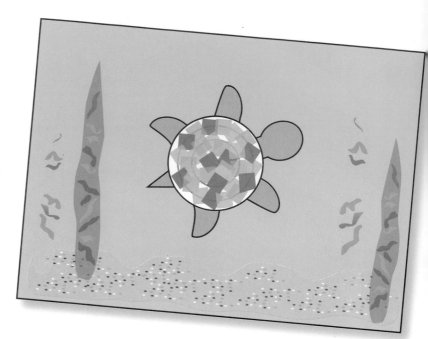

Materials for one:
12" x 18" sheet of light blue construction paper
glue
large box lid
sand
various shades of green tissue paper cut in
   2" strips (seaweed) and small squares
scissors
small paper bowl
green construction paper

To make one:
1. Spread glue along one long edge of the blue paper. Place the paper in the box lid. Sprinkle sand over the glue; then shake off the excess.
2. Glue seaweed to the paper. Scrunch the strips as you apply them to create a 3-D look.
3. Glue tissue paper squares all over the outside of the bowl to make the turtle's shell.
4. Cut turtle-head, tail, and flipper shapes from the green construction paper. Glue them to the rim of the bowl.
5. Glue the finished turtle to the center of the paper.

Marie Reed
Galloway Charter Kindergarten School
Smithville, NJ

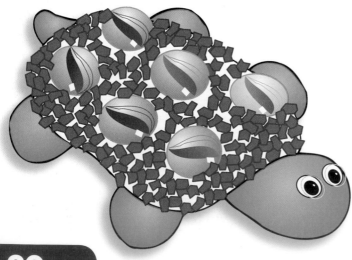

Tactile Turtles

Creating these turtles is a good way to use leftover craft supplies. Provide each child with a handful of Crayola Model Magic modeling compound. Challenge him to create a turtle. Then get out your remaining craft supplies and invite each child to use the materials to give his turtle's shell some texture. (Craft glue may need to be applied to some items before pushing them into the shell.) Allow the glue and modeling compound to dry. Then, if desired, use tempera paint or markers to color the turtle's head, feet, and tail. Finish the turtle by gluing on two wiggle-eye stickers.

Christine Guanipa
Covenant School
Arlington, MA

Shimmering Sharing

These colorful reminders about the importance of sharing are a real catch for your classroom windows! In advance, make several tagboard copies of the fish patterns on page 110 and cut them out. Then read aloud *The Rainbow Fish* by Marcus Pfister, a uniquely illustrated book about friendship and sharing. Afterward, invite each child to trace a fish pattern onto clear Con-Tact covering and then cut out the tracing. Instruct the child to remove (and discard) the paper backing. Then have her press a small piece of aluminum foil onto her fish to resemble a shiny scale. Next, have each child tear a piece of colorful tissue paper to resemble fish scales. Then encourage the child to share her tissue paper scales with other students, and vice versa, so that everyone has a variety of colors. Then have the child arrange her colorful collection of scales on her cutout until it is completely covered. Have the child use a permanent marker to draw an eye and mouth on her fish. Use clear tape to mount these fish onto your classroom windows for shimmering sharing reminders.

Teresa Shankle
Hospitots Preschool
Johnson City, TN

Splendid Fish Stamps!

Dive into the book *Swimmy* by Leo Lionni with these fabulous fish prints! In advance, collect a class supply of figure eight–shaped foam packing pieces. Cut the end off of each packing piece as shown. Provide students with access to stamp pads with red and black ink. To begin the activity, read *Swimmy* aloud. Then give each child a 12" x 18" sheet of white construction paper and a packing peanut. Instruct the child to draw a large fish on his paper. Next, have him ink a packing piece with red ink and then print fish shapes on his illustration as shown. Instruct each child to use the same process to print his fish's eye with black ink. When the ink is dry, direct each child to cut out his fish and then glue it onto a 12" x 18" sheet of blue construction paper. If desired, invite him to draw or paint other ocean-related items around his fish. This project is sure to make a splash!

Kim MacMullett
Philadelphia, PA

Bat Wing Patterns
Use with "Nighttime Neighbors"
on page 13.

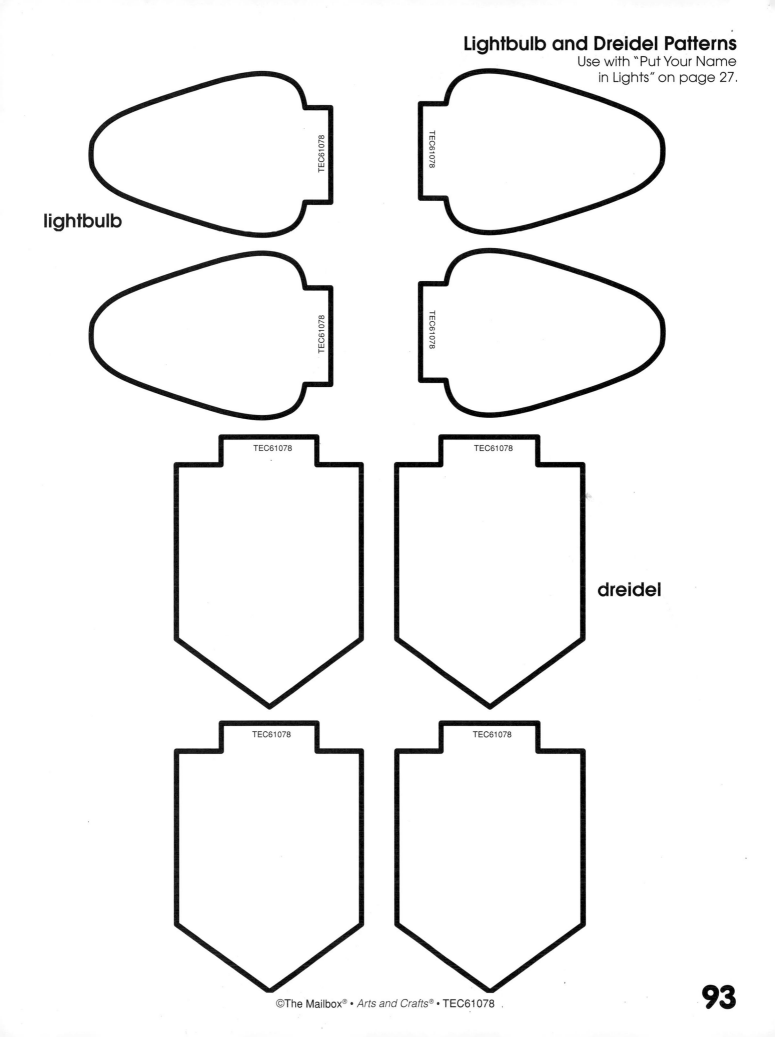

lightbulb

TEC61078

TEC61078

TEC61078

TEC61078

TEC61078

TEC61078

dreidel

TEC61078

TEC61078

Snowflake Stencil Pattern
Use with "Shimmering Snowflake" on page 30.

TEC61078

TEC61078

Bear Patterns
Use with "It's a Whiteout!" on page 34.

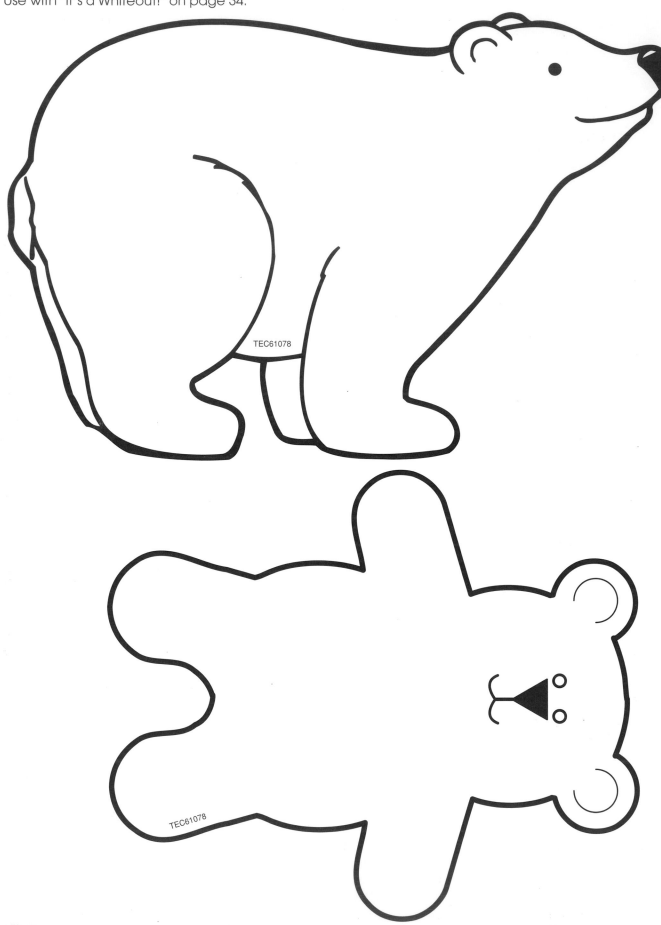

TEC61078

TEC61078

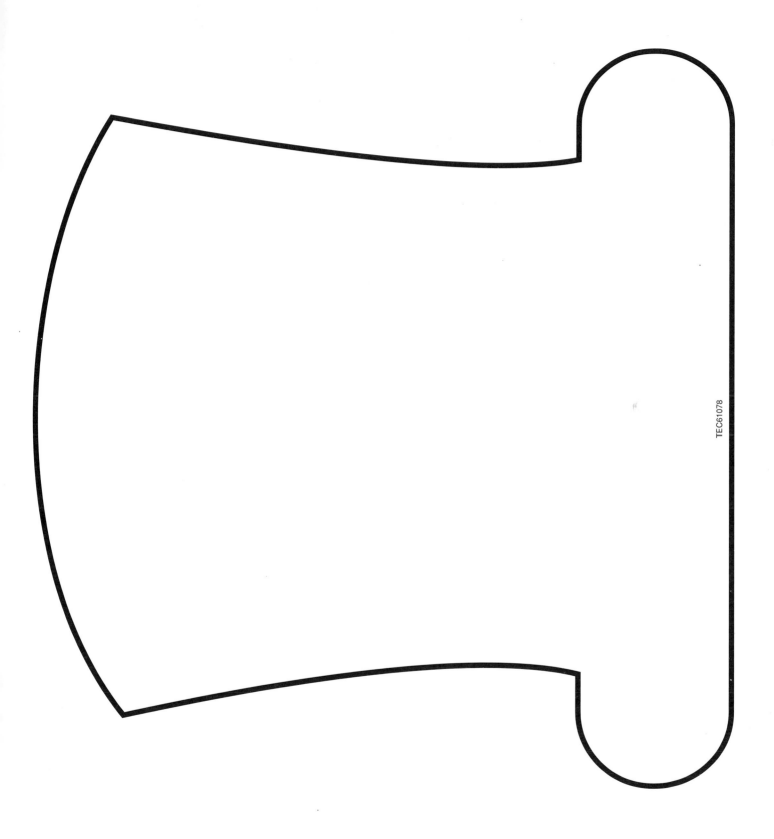

TEC61078

Rainbow Pattern
Use with "Lucky Rainbows" on page 47.

Glue yellow nuggets here.

Glue pot along this edge.

TEC61078

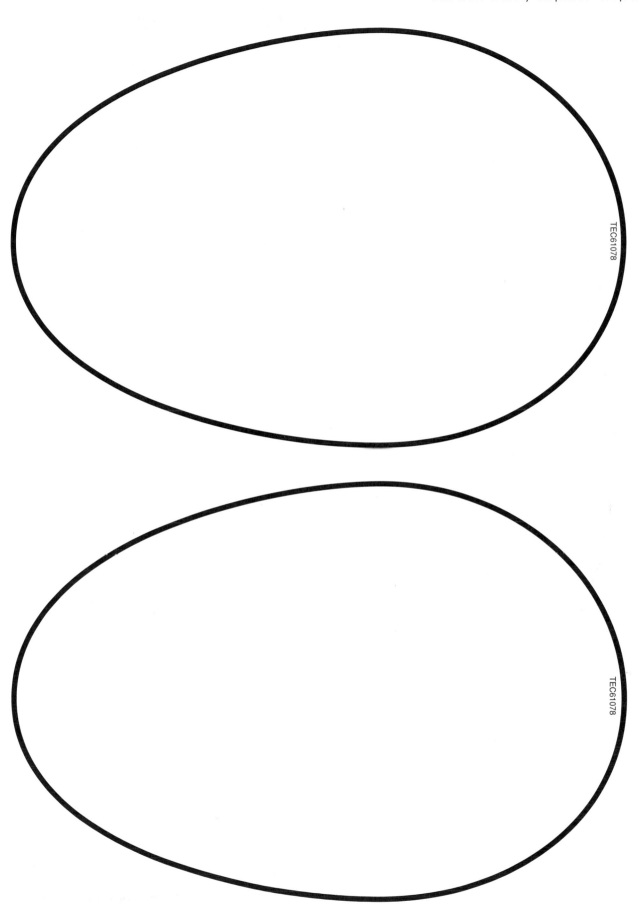

TEC61078

TEC61078

Mother's Day Poem

Use with "Garden in a Jar" on page 56.

I made this gift, Mom,
Just for you,
Because you're special
And I love you, too!
No need to water it,
For it can't grow.
It's just something
To let you know...
I'm thinking of you
On your special day!

Happy *Mother's Day!*

Hummingbird Body Patterns

Use with "Hurry-Scurry Hummingbirds" on page 58.

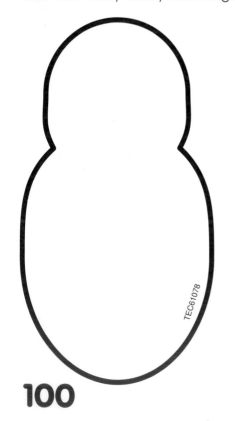
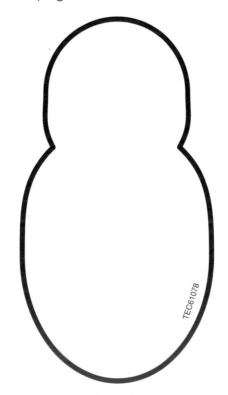
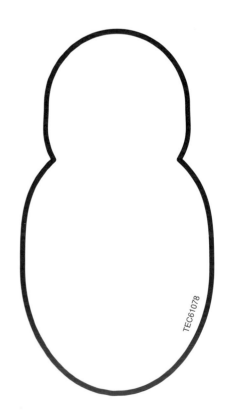

100

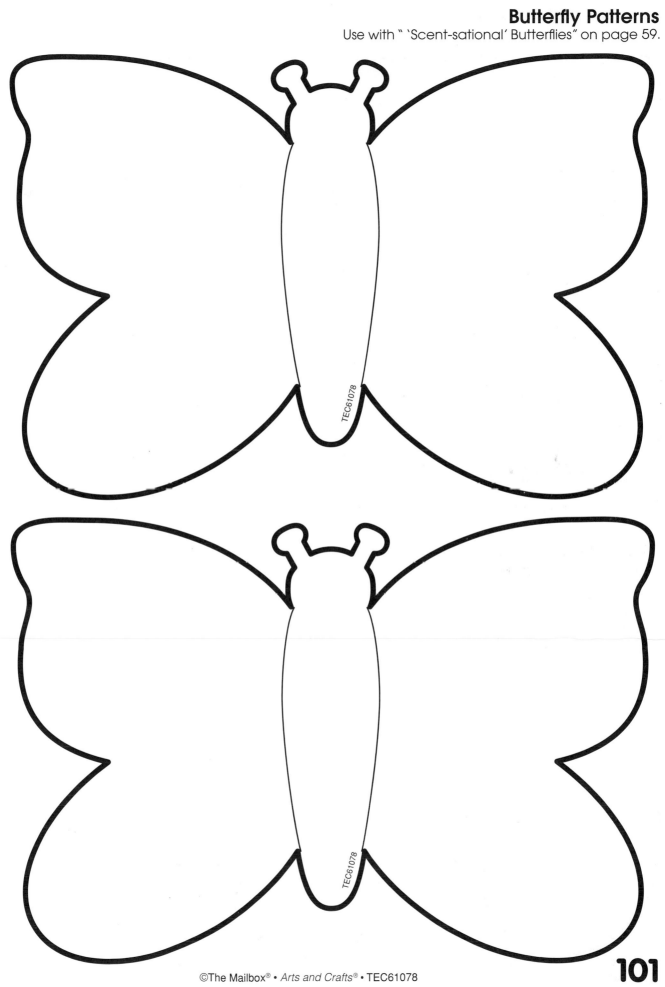

TEC61078

TEC61078

TEC61078

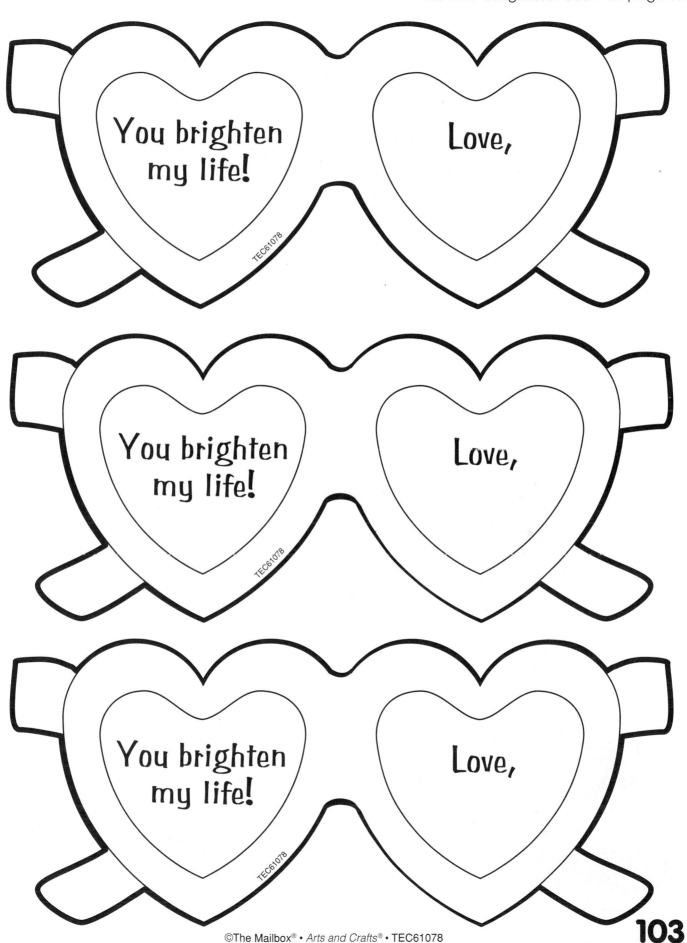

You brighten my life!

Love,

You brighten my life!

Love,

You brighten my life!

Love,

Pea Pod Patterns

Use with "Sweet Peas" on page 69.

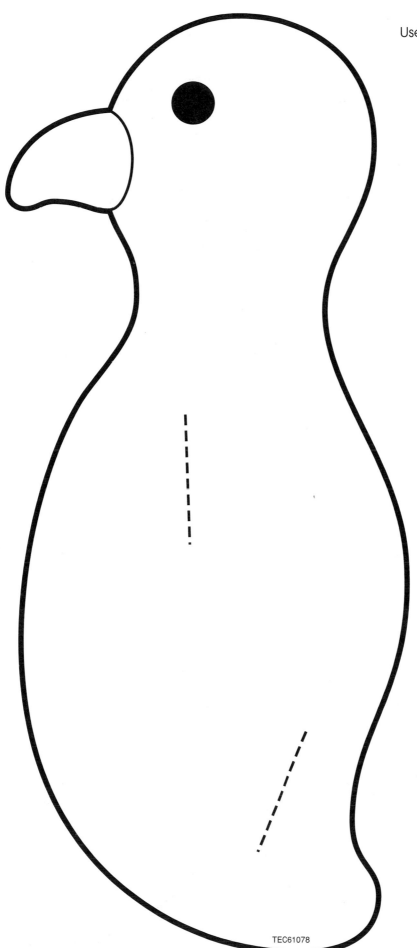

TEC61078

Carousel Pony Patterns
Use with "A Merry Carousel" on page 78.

TEC61078

TEC61078

TEC61078

TEC61078

TEC61078

TEC61078

TEC61078

Tyrannosaurus rex Outline and Skull Patterns
Use with "Tips for Making a *T. rex*" on page 80.

TEC61078

TEC61078

Fish Patterns
Use with "Shimmering Sharing" on page 91.

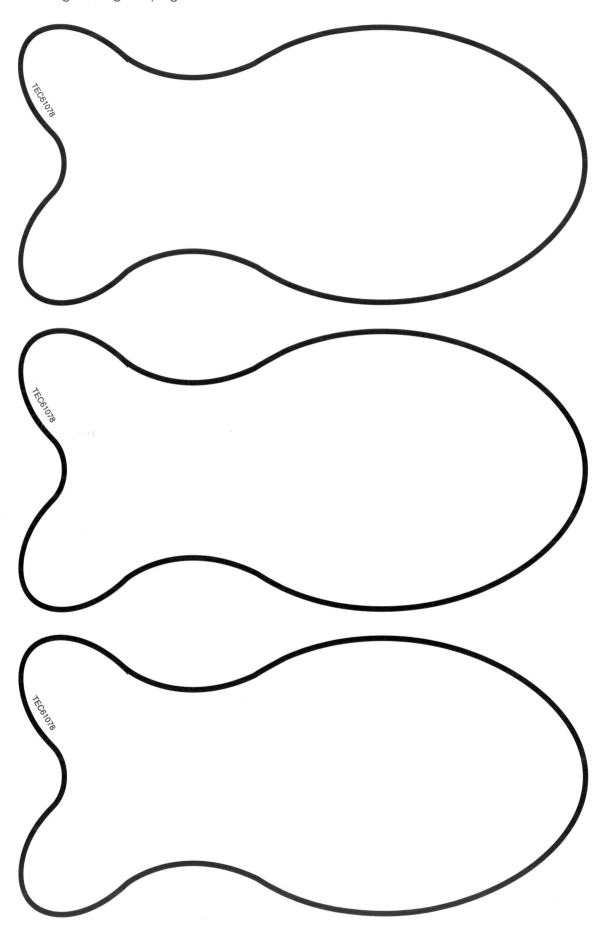

TEC61078

TEC61078

TEC61078

110

Index